10 ALARMING SERMONS SMOKING LIKE A VOLCANO

By

E. A. JOHNSTON

COVER PHOTO:

Author is seen standing in the pulpit at Hanham Mount, which commemorates the persecution of the Baptist community in the 1600s and the open-air preaching of John Wesley and George Whitfield, which started here in 1730s. Hanham was one of the first places that they preached in the open air.

DEDICATION

The following book of sermons is dedicated to two powerful preachers who greatly influenced me: my late pastor, Dr. Adrian Rogers, and my late homiletical mentor, Dr. Stephen Olford.

TABLE OF CONTENTS

INTRODUCTION

We live in a day of a "famine in the land" (Amos 8:11) for hearing the Word of God. Pulpits have become lecture and teaching podiums or entertainment platforms. Gone are the preachers of old who warned that sin is black and Hell is hot and a future judgment awaits all mankind!

Old Time preachers, full of the Holy Ghost, stood holding their Bible in one hand, and a stick of dynamite in the other, boldly proclaiming, "Thus saith the Lord!"

Preaching is to be transforming with the purpose of awakening sinners to their lost condition and alarming them to a perilous position of dying in their sins and entering a Christless eternity.

The Gospel of the Cross points lost souls to Calvary where a bloodstained Christ is the only remedy for sin.

The following ten sermons have been carefully selected out of two thousand sermons preached by noted evangelist, Dr. E. A. Johnston. Read them carefully and consider them solemnly for the good of your soul. Eternity hangs in the balance!

SERMON 1

LIKE MUSTARD ON A BLUE SUIT

Preached On: Sunday, November 10, 2024

Let me pray.

Great and terrible God in heaven, you are high and lifted up, whose name is holy. You dwell among the cherubim. Help me, I pray, Lord, to deliver this message that you have burning in my soul. I pray, great God, though Satan roar and hellish hosts revile forever, let me preach this message in the demonstration of the Spirit and of the power of God.

Bring a soul out of the kingdom of darkness into the kingdom of light and life. Open hearts, I pray, and reveal your Son as the pearl of great price who's worth selling all for and losing all for so he may be gained. For what profits a man if he gains the world, but loses his soul? There are some here tonight, Lord, who may be in danger of losing their soul. The devil's got four aces on them, their heart is as hard as a rock, but you say, Lord, in your word, that your word is a hammer that breaks the rock in pieces. And Lord, I ask you tonight to come and bust things up here. Bust up every false foundation of an empty religious profession. Bust up every false hope. Break apart every false refuge of carnal security. And Lord, there are people here sound asleep in their sins. You say that your word is like a fire, come burn someone's conscience in this message and awaken them to their lost condition and alarm them to their perilous position of dying in their sins and experiencing the terrible consequences of damnation in the devil's hell.

Great God, you also declare that your word is like a two-edged sword that divides asunder. I pray, great God, that by your Spirit you come here tonight and cut somebody up to pieces. Hew them down like Samuel hacked up old rotten King Agag. Open hearts tonight, I pray. Pull the curtains down on eternity. Let sinners tremble as they totter over the bottomless pit and dangle there like a worm being fed to a raven. Wake up these lost religious people, Lord, I pray. Save some of them before you remove them and send them to hell. You are a God who must punish sin. As those soldiers nailed up your Son, Jesus, to that cross, every stroke of the hammer was an exclamation point crying out, God must punish sin! God must punish sin! God must punish sin! Lord, I pray that your Spirit come among us and disturb folks. Let those here get a glimpse of heaven, hell, and eternity. I pray these things in the strong name of Jesus. Amen.

Well, let me gather myself a minute, friends. I plumb wore myself out here before I even got started. I've got a serious message for us this evening, friends, and it's a solemn warning, like the words of the prophet Jeremiah, "But his word was in my heart as a burning fire shut up in my bones." This message is burning in my bones, and I'm coming to you tonight, friends, like a smoking volcano erupting with warning. The hour is late and Christ's return is near. Like the apostle says, it is high time to awake out of sleep. The night is far spent. The day is at hand. Let us therefore cast off the works of darkness and put on the armor of light.

Do you believe, friends, that we're living in the last days? Do you believe we're living in dark days? Does it appear to you that the devil has the highway and society is in moral chaos and spinning out of control? Then why do you halt between two opinions, friend? If the Lord be God, follow him, but if Baal, then follow him. Baal was an idol that was just the face of the devil. The idol, your servant, friend, is really the devil. You can't play footsie with God in partial obedience. You're either 100% sold out to him or you're not. You can't have it both ways. You can't have one foot with God and one foot in the world. It's either God or Baal. You better settle this tonight, friend, or it'll be hell to pay.

I'm going to preach the unvarnished gospel to you tonight, friends, and like we say in the South, I'm going to give you the oil straight from the can. So sit up straight and get the wax out of your ears. God will do business tonight with those who want to do business with him.

I was playing golf with a giant of a man. He stood six foot five and was as wide as a brick wall, and every time this big man took a swing at the ball, he cursed God and cussed man. He had the filthiest mouth of any man I ever heard. I couldn't take it anymore, so finally I turned to him on a tee box and said, "Can I ask you a question?" He said, "Shoot." I said, "How is your relationship with God?" He smiled a big grin and said, "Fine, I have a great relationship with God. I leave him alone and he leaves me alone." That's what the big man said. Do you know what, friend? It breaks my heart to say it, all you have to do to go to hell is for God to leave you alone. If you're here tonight, and you are saved, it's because God gave you saving faith. Salvation is in the hands of God.

Well, that's my little introduction, friends. Let's get down to business. We've got a lot of ground to cover tonight. Let me share a story with you first. Years ago, I was preaching in a church down south in Mississippi one Sunday morning, and it was customary down south after the service was over to have a big smorgasbord for the visiting preacher. Well, we all went to the fellowship hall. We're at picnic tables. We're ready. In a long table, a buffet food was sitting there. Well, I like hot dogs, so I loaded up my plate with a few hot dogs, and I like mustard on my hot dogs; some of you kids might like mustard on your hot dogs as well. So I lathered them up from a jar of mustard on the table that was before me. I sat down with an old deacon and his wife, and I wondered why they were staring at me so, until I realized I had smeared yellow mustard all over the front of my brand new blue suit. The old deacon shook his head and said, "Well, at least we know you're human." I took that suit to the cleaners, but that mustard stain never came out of that blue suit. It always had a green hue. Every time after that, when I wore that suit and looked in the mirror, it always carried that stain and that's what sin does to you, friend. It stains you, and it won't come out. It won't come off of you. You can try to whitewash sin by calling it other names, but that won't do. A fib is still a lie. Taking something that doesn't belong to you is still stealing. Fooling around is still adultery. You can't whitewash sin by renaming it. Now listen to me, friends: sin is still sin, and it leaves a stain on you morally that you can't wash out, even by church membership. My new blue suit had that mustard stain, and it's still there, even though the suit is old.

The title of my message this evening, friends, is "Like Mustard On A Blue Suit," and my text can be found in the book of Revelation. You can turn in your Bibles there now, friends, we will be in chapter 20. I drink coffee when I have my quiet time with the Lord, and I keep my Bible in my lap, and I'm careful as to not spill any coffee, but one time I spilled coffee accidentally on a page of my Bible. Well, that brown stain never came out. Sin is like that in a book. God keeps a book on every one of us. In one day future, he will open the books and review our life, both the good and the bad. We see this to be the case in our text this evening from Revelation in chapter 20, beginning in verse 11.

> *11* And I saw a great white throne, and him that sat on it, from whose face the earth and the heaven fled away; and there was found no place for them.

Let me pause here, friends, to say this speaks of the final judgment of all mankind and the final dissolution of the whole frame of nature. That great white throne speaks of a tribulation of judgment. It's a heavenly courtroom scene. The white of that throne symbolizes purity and holiness of a thrice holy God. The judge of that throne is the judge of all the earth, and shall not the judge of all the earth do right? Well, let's take a look at who is appearing before that throne. Let's continue with our striking passage of Scripture.

> *12 And I saw the dead, small and great, stand before God; and the books were opened: and another book was opened, which is the book of life: and the dead were judged out of those things which were written in the books, according to their works.*

Let me pause here again, friends, to say, well, what books are these being referenced to? There's a book of remembrance that contains both good and bad. It's the detailed biography of our life. God will open the books on us. The next book is the book of God's law and each man will be held up against the strictness and severity of God's unbending law and all will fail that test for all have sinned and come short of the glory of God.

Those guilty lawbreakers will face the intense scrutiny of that judge. Then, there is a book that decides one's eternal destiny, the book of life. Well, this heavenly courtroom scene where cases will be reviewed and evidence presented and examined, every word, every thought, every deed will be reviewed by the one who has eyes of fire.

Well, let's continue with our text, friends.

13 And the sea gave up the dead which were in it; and death and hell delivered up the dead which were in them: and they were judged every man according to their works. 14 And death and hell were cast into the lake of fire. This is the second death. 15 And whosoever was not found written in the book of life was cast into the lake of fire.

I will stop there. Oh, what a solemn scene. It's a courtroom scene and if I may so speak, where the Son of God is the judge, the angels are the bailiffs, and Satan is the prosecuting attorney, the accuser, the brethren. All of mankind stands there from every generation since Adam, who will be justified and acquitted by the judge, those whose names are found written in the Book of Life. There stands before that judge a vast crowd of people. There stands the antediluvians of Noah's day who rejected the preaching of Noah and who drowned in the flood. There stands the men of Sodom, who mocked righteous Lot, and of whom God rained fire and hell out of heaven and consumed them. There stands the Jewish religious leaders who shouted, "Crucify him!" There stands Pontius Pilate, who now himself is being judged by the one he judged. There stands the Caesars. There stands the kings and queens. There stands the potentates of every nation. There stands the presidents and leaders of every nation, from every continent, in every generation. There stands the rich and the poor, the famous and the unknown, the movers and the shakers, the small and the great. There stand your co-workers. There stand your neighbors.

There stand your friends and family members. They face that righteous judge with the heat of that lake of fire burning behind them as it spits and spews and sizzles and torments those who are bound hand and foot and cast in there for all eternity.

How about you friend? How about you? How will you stand? Will you stand there with mustard on your blue suit with the stain of sin upon you? Will it be too late for change then, friend? I believe it'll be too late then, for as a tree falls, so it shall lay.

> *11 He that is unjust, let him be unjust still: and he which is filthy, let him be filthy still: and he that is righteous, let him be righteous still: and he that is holy, let him be holy still.*

Like mustard on a blue suit, your sins will find you out. You'll be too late then, friend, and like mustard on a blue suit, you'll be found guilty of the stain of sin and breaking God's law and the sentencing of the law will be carried out by that judge who sits behind that pure great white throne as he announces the sentence against you.

> *13 Then said the king to the servants, Bind him hand and foot, and take him away, and cast him into outer darkness; there shall be weeping and gnashing of teeth.*

The suffering of the damned in hell is spoken of here. Weeping speaks of great loss and grief. Gnashing the teeth signifies great anger and regret. I speak to you tonight, friend, about the dangers of damnation in the devil's hell. Let me read you the verse that precedes the striking passage of scripture about this great white throne judgment. In Revelation 20:10, we read,

> *10 And the devil that deceived them was cast into the lake of fire and brimstone, where the beast and the false prophet are, and shall be tormented day and night for ever and ever.*

Do you want to be that destiny friend? Do you want that to be you? Will you admit that you're in danger? Will you admit that you're a guilty sinner? Will you admit that you've been hiding in the church for years under a profession of faith? Will you admit that your hope of heaven is as empty as a hole in the wall? Will you turn to Christ now and repent of your sins? You're not in hell yet, friend. There is still time. There's still time to repent and surrender to God. Listen to God now as he declares,

> *18 Come now, and let us reason together, saith the LORD: though your sins be as scarlet, they shall be as white as snow; though they be red like crimson, they shall be as wool.*

Like mustard on a blue suit, sin stains the soul. Only the blood of Christ can wash away the stain of sin. You must be born from above, then washed in the blood, friend. If you've not trusted this blessed Savior, receive him now before it's too late. Soon he will come in judgment on this world when his anger shall burn as an oven and then you shall meet him as your judge. Turn to God, friend, before it's too late. Surrender your all to him. Jesus gave his all on Calvary, holding nothing back. How can you hold anything back from him? Come to Jesus. Come. What are you waiting for, mister? Don't wait until you're better. Come. Bring to him your heartache. Bring to him your tears. Come. Come to Jesus. The gospel is for the weary, the hungry, and the thirsty. You must feel your need of a Savior for sin. Listen to this final gospel call.

> *17 And the Spirit and the bride say, Come. And let him that heareth say, Come. And let him that is athirst come. And whosoever will, let him take the water of life freely.*

Listen, friends, the very last words of Jesus recorded in the book of Revelation are these, "Surely I come quickly."

"When Jesus steps out

I hear the sound of a mighty rushing wind And it's closer now than it's ever been

I can almost hear the trumpet as Gabriel sounds the chord At the midnight cry we'll be going home.

When Jesus steps out on a cloud to call his children The dead in Christ shall rise to meet him in the air And then those that remain will be quickly changed At the midnight cry when Jesus comes again."

SERMON 2

GOD OF THE BIBLE VS YOUR GOD

Preached On: Thursday, October 31, 2024

I have a solemn message for us today, friends, so you better get the wax out of your ears and sit up straight and pay attention. I'm not here to entertain you or make you laugh. I'm here to warn you of your danger. Many of you are well familiar with the passage from 1 Kings about the prophet Elijah and the contents of the prophets of Baal, which took place on top Mount Carmel. Well, Elijah had old wicked King Ahab assemble all the children of Israel together at Mount Carmel and he addressed them and said, "How long halt ye between two opinions? If the Lord be God, follow him, but if Baal, then follow him." And the people answered him not a word. They stood there guilty with their mouths shut because they knew in their hearts they'd been playing footsie with God, serving him with their lips and with their religious ceremonies, but really serving Baal with their lives and worshiping idols for material gain. The Jews in the days of Elijah were following a false god, an idol made of wood, made of stone, a dead god who could neither hear nor talk.

The Jews were serving Baal because they believed he was in control of the weather, and he gave them fair crops, gave them their material wealth. It came from serving him. They served Baal for selfish reasons.

Many serve a false god today, friends, out of selfish reasons as well but they don't want to go to hell. Still, others serve a false god out of ignorance. Did you know you can be religious and lost? Did you know you can be religious and misled? Did you know you can be religious and in ignorance? Let me share the final and true story with you, please. pay attention to it. A missionary shared the following story. He said, you could stand on a cliff in Mexico and gaze down at a certain village of Mexican workers. These people work down in the riverbed in their corn patch, and there they grow their corn. And when the corn is ready to harvest, they shuck it and after it dries out they'll take it and grind it into cornmeal and make tortillas and then take these tortillas down to the open market and there sell the tortillas for a few pesos and put them away. Come back out to their house and there they will live off lizards. They'll go out among the rocks and catch these huge long lizards and they'll eat those lizards and save that money for a special day, a special day when they will start a pilgrimage up a mountain to a wooden statue of Jesus. The terrain to that statue is so bad that most of the people will have to crawl on their hands and knees half a mile, and by the time they get to that statue, they're bleeding all over. Standing beside the statue is a priest, and that priest is saying, "Now, you love God, give to him, because you show your love to God by giving." And those people will reach into their little bags and purses and pull out those pesos stained in their own blood and drop that money into a slit in the top of the head of Jesus. Then the priest prays, and when he is finished, the priest will yell, "You have not given enough! Look, Jesus is sad. He is crying." And all the time, there will be another priest hidden in that hollow statue and with a little hand pump, he will pump water to where it comes out of human-made tear ducts and that statue is crying. And there, those people will give all they have, crawl down that mountain, and go back to eating lizards growing their corn, to make more tortillas, to get more pesos, to go and give to a dead god that cannot move or hear.

Now that's a pretty sad and tragic story, isn't it, friends, but I submit to you, friends, that there are some here, within the sound of my voice, who are serving a God of their own creation. Somewhere, they got out their pocket knives and have carved out for themselves a god they can live with, a god of their own imagination, that won't get in the way of their daily living, and that's the majority of the church right now.

Well, that's the end of my little introduction, friends. Let's get down to cases. Today, I will present the evidence of the true and the false. It is up to you to decide and come to a conclusion. I will present the evidence of the true God of the Bible and ask you for a verdict, "If God be God, then follow him. If Baal, then follow him." It is time for the rubber to meet the road. It's time to own up to our false delusions and danger of dying in our sins. It's time to stop wasting God's time that he gave us in the accumulation of wood, hay, and stubble by chasing the world. It's time to go for the gold, the silver, and the precious stones that will survive the fire of testing. It's time to get serious with God. God gets serious with those who get serious with him. The bottom line is, do you want to follow the true God and go to heaven with Jesus or do you want to follow a false God and end up in hell with the devil? This is a solemn sermon for serious listeners. It's time to stop playing games with God, friend. It's time to stop sinning against God and still call yourself a Christian. It's time for obedience to God. It's time for holiness unto the Lord.

He won't come back for a dirty bride. It's time for the people of God to get their house in order and to walk with God in obedience and in the fear of him.

My sermon today is in two parts. The first part is about the true God of the Bible, the living God of the word.

The second part of my message, friends, is about the word of God, what is it and how do you know when you've heard it? Let those who have ears to hear, may this message be a savor of life to some or a savor of death to others. The title of my message today friends is "The True God Versus Your God." We will be in the book of Jeremiah. You can turn in your Bibles there now, friends. We will be in chapter 23.

We will begin reading in verse 11. Here now is the word of God. May the Spirit of the Lord attend the reading of his holy word.

> *11 For both prophet and priest are profane; yea, in my house have I found their wickedness, saith the LORD. 12 Wherefore their way shall be unto them as slippery ways in the darkness: they shall be driven on, and fall therein: for I will bring evil upon them, even the year of their visitation, saith the LORD.*

I will pause here to say, friends, God just announced he will bring evil upon all religious leaders who are lying prophets. God will punish them. You know, a lot of people today don't believe in a God who will punish sin. If you took a survey in your average Baptist church today and ask the question, "Do you believe God will send you to hell," most folks would be offended by that remark, most folks would not agree with you because most folks don't believe their God would send anybody to hell unless it was a serial killer or a sociopath. Many today don't recognize the God of the Old Testament because their God is all love, their God is a big Santa Claus god, full of mercy and compassion, and that's it, no justice; their god is a sin-tolerating god. But guess what, friends? Jesus never preached a sin and religion. Their god has been shrunken down to their level to think and act like they do but the word of God says of God in Isaiah, "For my thoughts are not your thoughts, neither are your ways my ways, saith the LORD. For as the heavens are higher than the earth, so are my ways higher than your ways, and my thoughts than your thoughts." But many in our churches today are unfamiliar with the God of the Bible; that's because they never read their Bibles or even spend time to get to know God.

Unfortunately, many of our church leaders today are run by men, men who don't know God. In our text, in Jeremiah chapter 23, we read in verses 16 through 17,

> *16 Thus saith the LORD of hosts, Hearken not unto the words of the prophets that prophesy unto you: they make you vain: they speak a vision of their own heart, and not out of the mouth of the LORD. 17 They say still unto them that despise me, The LORD hath said, Ye shall have peace; and they say unto every one that walketh after the imagination of his own heart, No evil shall come upon you.*

Well, I will pause here, friends, to say, sadly, people are in churches run by men who don't know God. They were never called of God into the ministry. They are false shepherds speaking lies in words of comfort when they should be warning you to flee from the wrath to come. They represent a false god.

Many believe in a false god today, a god of their own making, like those Mexican workers, because of ignorance. Many also serve a god of their own imagination because of ignorance. Their god would never judge a nation for its sins by sending remedial judgments to them in the form of natural calamities like fires and floods and pestilence.

Their pastors just soothe them saying, "No evil should come upon you." And taken to the extreme, this can be universalism. Like a lady I knew in church, back when Michael Jackson died, I heard her say that he was in heaven. I asked her why in the world did she think Michael Jackson was in heaven? And she said, "Well, he's in heaven." I said, "Why? He never claimed to be a Christian. Why was he in heaven if he lived such an ungodly life?" And this is what this woman said to me, she said that she believed after we die, Jesus comes to us and gives us all a chance to go to heaven. That's the god she believed in, and it was detrimental to her, for eventually she took her own life, assuming she'd just get a second chance on the other side.

It's dangerous not to believe in the God of the Bible, friends. If you follow the wrong god, he'll lead you straight to a devil's hell. Man must know the God of the Bible versus the god of their imaginations. Man must know the one true God of the word of God. God declares in Jeremiah 23:21 through 22,

> *21 I have not sent these prophets, yet they ran: I have not spoken to them, yet they prophesied. 22 But if they had stood in my counsel, and had caused my people to hear my words, then they should have turned them from their evil way, and from the evil of their doings.*

This leads us to the second part of my message today, friends, on what is the word of God, and how do we know when you have heard faithful preaching. Notice the last part of verse 22 contains the answer to our question; had these prophets preached the truth of God's word, there would have been a reaction from the hearers, and that would have been repentance and reformation, they'd be turned from their evil way and evil doings. So secondly, men must know the word of God. Well, what is the word of God? Look at Jeremiah 23 and verses 28 and 29, and let's see what God says.

> *28 The prophet that hath a dream, let him tell a dream; and he that hath my word, let him speak my word faithfully. What is the chaff to the wheat? saith the LORD. 29 Is not my word like as a fire? saith the LORD; and like a hammer that breaketh the rock in pieces?*

Well, let me ask you, friend, what does a fire do? It awakens and alarms. If your family is asleep in your home and a fire breaks out in the night and the smoke alarms go off, you're awakened to your danger. You'll get up, you'll run and get your loved ones out to safety. If you see the flames, you are alarmed to your danger. So the preached word of God, when faithfully proclaimed, will be as a fire to awaken one to their lost condition; outside of Christ, it would be like a fire to alarm them of their perilous position of dying in their sins. A fire throws light on a situation. When God is barbecuing me, I know it, and I must get my life in proper order.

Well, let me ask you this, friends: what does a hammer do? It pounds away on something. It drives a nail in. It penetrates something. It busts something up. When the word of God is faithfully proclaimed, God's word will fall with the weight of a heavy hammer and bust up any and every false foundation of carnal security and bust up every empty religious profession.

So God describes his word as a fire and a hammer. Well, what else does he say about his word? In Hebrews

4:12, God describes his word as a sword, "For the word of God is quick, and powerful, and sharper than any twoedged sword, piercing even to the dividing asunder of soul and spirit, and of the joints and marrow, and is a discerner of the thoughts and intents of the heart." Oh, what does a sword do? It cuts to pieces like Samuel hewing King Agag down with a double-edged claymore. I used to have an exact replica of a claymore sword. It was so big and heavy I had to hold it in two hands. You could really cut somebody up with that thing if it was sharp enough. So the word of God is like a sharp sword that penetrates the hard heart and cuts the sinner to pieces, bringing conviction to sin. Like the men at Pentecost who heard Peter's powerful sermon, they were pierced through and through. In Acts 2:37 we read, "Now when they heard this, they were pricked in their heart, and said unto Peter and to the rest of the apostles, Men and brethren, what shall we do?" Well, what did Peter tell them? "Repent, and be baptized every one of you in the name of Jesus Christ for the remission of sins, and ye shall receive the gift of the Holy Ghost."

So the word of God is a fire, a hammer, a sword, and you can recognize when you've heard it preached faithfully when a result occurs in either conviction or transformation. Well, what is the result of the preached word of God? Not to entertain, but to transform, to bring repentance, reformation, conviction, and salvation through Christ Jesus. So men must know the God of the word. Men must know the word of God. 1 Corinthians 2:4 declares, "And my speech and my preaching was not with enticing words of man's wisdom, but in demonstration of the Spirit and of power:" But the word of God, friends, must be preached by the Spirit of God in the power of God to bring transformation, and to get that anointing for the preacher there is a cost. What cost counts and what counts costs. The cost is death to self via the cross.

J. Sidlow Baxter used to say, "How can a man full of himself preach a Christ who emptied himself?" If you are a God-called pastor, preacher, evangelist, missionary, or Christian worker, it's time to stop playing footsie with the world and go all out on the full stretch for God. Jesus held nothing back at Calvary but gave all of himself to be nailed up there on that bloody cross. How can we hold anything back from him?

This is the time, friends, for rededication. This is the time, friends, for repentance and reformation. It is time to get serious with the God of the Bible. It's time to surrender to the Lord Jesus Christ, to surrender all to him. Let us come to him now and do business with God. Listen friends, get serious with him right now.

"Love sent my Savior to die in my stead; Why should He love me so?

Meekly to Calvary's cross He was led; Why should He love me so?

Why should He love me so? Why should He love me so?

Why should my Savior to Calvary go? Why should He love me so?

Nails pierced His hands and His feet for my sin; Why should He love me so?

He suffered sore my salvation to win: Why should He love me so?

Why should He love me so? Why should He love me so?

Why should my Savior to Calvary go? Why should He love me so?"

SERMON 3

3 WORDS HAUNT IN HELL: SIN IS COSTLY

Preached On: Sunday, December 20, 2015

I believe there are three words which will haunt you in hell and I believe these three words are being shouted in hell tonight. The cries of the damned are encircled around these three terrible words. Listen to me, friends, if you die in your sins and you are cast into hell's fire, the three words will follow you there, three words will gnaw at you there. The three words which will haunt you in hell are these: sin is costly. Sin is costly. Sin is costly. That's what the doomed are crying right now. That's what the wicked are screaming right now. That's what the damned in hell are hollering right now. Sin is costly! Sin is costly! Sin is costly!

That's the title of my message this evening, friends, "Sin Is Costly," and my text can be found in the book of Numbers 32. You can turn in your Bibles there now, friends. It's just one little verse, but that one verse will follow you into hell. Look at verse 23,

> *23 But if ye will not do so, behold, ye have sinned against the LORD: and be sure your sin will find you out.*

While I was writing the authorized biography of J. Sidlow Baxter, I learned of his conversion. While he was a young man in England, Sidlow Baxter just loved detective stories and while walking one day down the street in Manchester, he saw a sign over a theater advertising an evangelistic crusade and the sign said, "The Infallible Detective," and Sidlow said to himself, "My, I must go and hear that." And he did, and the evangelist preached a message from Numbers 32:23 on this infallible detective from the verse, "your sin will find you out." And it's true, friends, your sin will find you out. You may think you can hide from God's eyes as you hug yours sins and indulge your flesh, but his eye is constantly upon you. The infallible detective is at your heels tonight, friends.

I want to take a walk with you now through the Bible as we look at our theme this evening of the 3 words which will haunt you in hell, sin is costly, and I want to explore this theme with the following divisions. 1. How sin will cost you in life. 2. How sin will cost you in eternity, and I have several subdivisions attached as we proceed. You may want to get out your pens and paper and take notes as you take note of this frightening message on sin and its ramifications, sin is costly.

I was having a conversation recently with a fellow evangelist. He's a veteran evangelist who has been preaching for several decades and he has a close walk with God and he was sharing with me a sad story about his father. He said his father was a pastor who had fallen into moral failure and committed adultery. He lost his church. He lost his reputation. He lost it all for eventually this former pastor became homeless. Then my friend looked away to the distance and his eyes became sad as he related this tragic story to me as a warning to every one of us and he made the following comment. He said, "Sin is costly," and I chewed on that for a while and his words stuck with me for several days, sin is costly, for I know for a fact that it is, and I could not let loose of those 3 striking words without putting them into this message tonight, this message which should be a solemn warning to all who hear it. Sin is costly. Those 3 words will follow you into hell.

Those 3 words will haunt you in hell forever and ever and ever. Sin is costly.

I wish to begin the sermon with the aspect of how sin will cost you in life and I believe the proof text for this can be found in one of the saddest chapters in my Bible, 2 Samuel

11. Turn in your Bibles there now, friends, as we peer into the life of a man favored by God who carelessly and presumptuously sinned against God and that man was King David. We find David reclining and resting on his recent successes when he should have been out fighting the Lord's battles. He rises from his bed and goes for a stroll atop his palace and his eyes fall upon a stunning beauty who was washing herself. She is naked and he should have looked away, but instead he leered, he lusted, and he began his great descent into the sins of adultery and murder. Listen to me, friend, sin will always take you further than you want to go. It will leave you there longer than you want to stay and it will cost you more than you ever realized. Our text in verse 2 reads,

> *"And it came to pass in an eveningtide, that David arose from off his bed, and walked upon the roof of the king's house: and from the roof he saw a woman washing herself; and the woman was very beautiful to look upon."*

Now I want to have you turn over in your Bibles, friends, as we scan the price that King David paid for his sin, the consequence of his sin, the cost of his sin in his life. In chapter 13 of 2 Samuel, we find the record of Amnon raping Tamar, then Absalom kills Amnon for this wicked act. Then in chapter 15, verse 13 we read, "The hearts of the men of Israel are after Absalom." David's choice son has turned against him in rebellion. Then Absalom is killed and we see David's heart break from the news of his son's death. Listen to the anguish in his voice as found in 2 Samuel 18:33, "And the king was much moved, and went up to the chamber over the gate, and wept: and as he went, thus he said, O my son Absalom, my son, my son Absalom! would God I had died for thee, O Absalom, my son, my son!" This, friends, is a clear picture of the certain fact that sin is costly. Sin will cost you in life. David's sin affected his entire family.

I once knew a man who had a perfect life. He had a lovely home, a good job, an affectionate Christian wife and several beautiful children. He served in several capacities of leadership at his church. Then he got a new young secretary who was half his age, and he had an adulterous affair with her. His sin cost him his family, for his marriage ended in divorce. He lost his house. He lost his reputation as a Christian leader. One of his children rebelled in her teenage years and her life became a train wreck. Listen to me, friend, and listen to me very carefully: sin will cost you in life. It will ruin your marriage. It will ruin your home. It will ruin your family. Do you believe that? Do you?

Listen to me, brother pastor, sin will cost you in ministry. How many men have I known through the years in ministry who have fallen into grievous sin and it wrecked their church, it wrecked their ministry. Sin will cost you in life. If you want to pick a fight with me on that one, I believe you'll lose because in the end your sin will find you out. You may be able to hide it now, brother, you may be able to hide it now, sister, but you cannot hide from the one who has eyes afire, a holy God. Your sin will find you out. Sin will cost you in life. I can promise you that. You cannot escape the ramifications and consequence of sin.

If you don't believe me, friend, just go through your Bible and begin in the book of Genesis and see how sin ruined the human race, how sin put man under a curse. Every mother's son born into this world drinks iniquity like it's water. That's because of his natural inclination, because his ruined nature is drawn to sin. God spewed out the following bitter words to Adam, "Cursed is the ground for thy sake. In sorrow shalt thou eat of it all the days of thy life." Sin will cost you in life, friend, you can count on that and that's not my saying it, that is a holy God saying it who hates all sin.

Come with me now to peer more deeply into how sin ruins mankind. God told Cain, "Sin lieth at the door," and we see the first murder take place as Cain kills his brother Abel.

Then we see how costly sin is, friends, as sin destroys an entire world, an entire race, save one family which was Noah's family. In Genesis 6:5-6 we read, "And GOD saw that the wickedness of man was great in the earth, and that every imagination of the thoughts of his heart was only evil continually. And it repented the LORD that he had made man on the earth, and it grieved him at his heart." Sin will cost you in this life, friend. Sin is costly. Sin is costly. Sin is costly.

Now, I wish to explore this next aspect with you of our great theme tonight and that is, 2. sin will cost you in eternity. I really believe, friends, that the 3 words you will hear in hell, the 3 words which will follow you into hell, the 3 words which will haunt you continually in hell are these: sin is costly. Sin is costly. Sin is costly. That's the cry of the damned as they gnash their teeth together in deep regret.

Listen to me, friend: if I could walk you right now

over to the precipice of hell and lift the lid off that bottomless pit, I believe you'd hear millions and millions of lost souls crying out in agony tonight, "Sin is costly! Don't come here to this place of torment! Listen to our warnings! Sin is costly! Sin is costly! It cost me my soul. I can't get out of this horrible prison. Listen to me, those of you still on the earth, don't come to this place of torment and misery! Sin is costly! Sin is costly! Sin is costly!" That is their cry, friend.

Will it be your cry as well?

Now, let me explore a final aspect of our theme this evening and it is this: sin cost a holy God his only begotten Son and sin cost Jesus Christ his precious blood. Mark 15:25 records the result of the cost of sin. Listen to these stark words which cause the angels in heaven to pause and weep, "And it was the third hour, and they crucified him." Listen to me, friend, the little god you serve in this life won't serve you too well in eternity. You'd better trade out your little god of your imagination, the little god who lets you have a salvation and still be comfortable in sin. Listen to me: you'd better get rid of that god, friend, for he will surely cost you in hell because God must punish sin. The God of the Bible must punish sin.

Now, some of you don't believe that, your God wouldn't act that way, but the God of the Bible would. God will and must punish sin. Sin costs. And when they took the Lord of glory with cruel hands, when they took that innocent blood and nailed him to that horrible death instrument of the cross, when the Roman soldiers took that hammer in their hands and began to pound and drive those thick nails into the Savior's tender hands, every blow of the hammer was an exclamation point of, "God must punish sin! God must punish sin! God must punish sin!"

Look at me, friend, give me your undivided attention. Listen to what I'm saying to you right now. All of you within the sound of my voice, listen to these 3 words and listen to them loud and clear: sin is costly. Sin will cost you in life. Sin will cost you in eternity. Sin is costly! Sin is costly! Sin is costly! Jesus said, "Unless you repent, ye shall all likewise perish," and that means you, friend, even if you're the Chairman of the Deacons.

I'm going to take a moment to preach the Gospel to you and it is my prayer, friends, that you won't hear this poor preacher's shaky voice so much, but that you will hear his voice as it comes to you in all power, authority, and majesty. Listen to the following pleas of the Gospel as they ring in your ears right now.

> *"Seek ye the LORD while he may be found, call ye upon him while he is near: Let the wicked forsake his way, and the unrighteous man his thoughts: and let him return unto the LORD, and he will have mercy upon him; and to our God, for he will abundantly pardon."*

> *"All that the Father giveth me shall come to me; and him that cometh to me I will in no wise cast out."*

> *"Look unto me, and be ye saved, all the ends of the earth: for I am God, and there is none else."*

> *"Come unto me, all ye that labour and are heavy laden, and I will give you rest. Take my yoke upon you, and learn of me; for I am meek and lowly in heart: and ye shall find rest unto your souls. For my yoke is easy, and my burden is light."*

"And the Spirit and the bride say, Come. And let him that heareth say, Come. And let him that is athirst come. And whosoever will, let him take the water of life freely."

SERMON 4

DAY LATE AND A DOLLAR SHORT

Preached On: Saturday, September 28, 2024

My message tonight, friends, is a solemn warning. 284 years ago, in the pulpits of America, it was not uncommon to hear the ministers of New England preach sermons that were solemn warnings to their hearers. God used those searching sermons full of the Holy Ghost, full of the doctrines of grace, to bring revivals. One thinks of Jonathan Edwards and his sermon, "Sinners in the Hands of an Angry God," which he preached in Enfield, Connecticut on July 8, 1741, where an eyewitness recorded in his diary of that event.

"We went over to Enfield, where we met dear Mr. Edwards of Northampton, who preached a most awakening sermon from these words, Deuteronomy 32:35, '

> *To me belongeth vengeance, and recompence; their foot shall slide in due time: for the day of their calamity is at hand, and the things that shall come upon them make haste.'*

And before the sermon was done, there was a great moaning and crying out through the whole house

—'What shall I do to be saved?'; 'Oh, I am going to hell!'; 'Oh, what shall I do for Christ?' etc. To where the minister was obliged to desist from preaching. The shrieks and cries were piercing and amazing."

Well, we don't hear much searching sermons today, friends, that are solemn warnings to the unconverted.

Instead, we preach nice little messages that don't disturb a flea or the deacons, yet alone convert a sinner from his ways. And because of our politically correct pulpits today, we don't see any revivals either. But things have gotten so bad in society and so bad in the church it's time to take the meat-axe out and hew down some sinners.

I need to pray before I preach to you tonight, friends, because I can't do this alone. I've got too much coming against me. I need God's Spirit upon me and I need Christ's disturbing presence among us. That's my prayer. That's my hope. That's my need. Let me pray.

O great and terrible God, you dwell among the cherubim. Turn your face toward us, Lord, this evening, and walk among us, I pray, with your divine presence; by your Spirit, come and disturb folks, I pray. If anyone here is resting upon an empty religious profession, I pray you take your word, and like a hammer, bust that thing to pieces. Let your word be as a fire that awakens and alarms and singes the very conscience. Make your word a meat-axe to hew sinners down like Samuel hacked King Agag to pieces. If there's someone here whose faith is as empty as a hole in the wall, then smoke them out of their false refuge. I pray these things in the strong name of Jesus. Amen.

If you brought a Bible with you tonight, friends, turn to the gospel of Matthew; in chapter 25, we would deal tonight with the parable of the wise and foolish virgins. Here now is the word of God. May the Spirit of the Lord attend the reading of his holy word. This is Jesus talking,

> *1 Then shall the kingdom of heaven be likened unto ten virgins, which took their lamps, and went forth to meet the bridegroom. 2 And five of them were wise, and five were foolish. 3 They that were*

foolish took their lamps, and took no oil with them: 4 But the wise took oil in their vessels with their lamps. 5 While the bridegroom tarried, they all slumbered and slept. 6 And at midnight there was a cry made, Behold, the bridegroom cometh; go ye out to meet him.

Well, let me pause here, friends, to say it was a custom among the Jews that the bridegroom came, attended with his friends, late in the night, to the house of the bride, where she expected him, attended with her bridesmaids, who, upon notice given of the bridegroom's approach, were to go out with lamps in their hands to light the way for him into the house. The bridegroom is our Lord Jesus Christ, who at present is tarrying his return. Right now, that bridegroom is tarrying, but he will come as a thief in the night when you least expect it, meaning he could come any time now. Are you prepared to meet him? Our text says the five foolish virgins were not prepared. They were unprepared. Oh, friends, listen to me. All these women were professed believers. They were like members of a church each believing they had an assurance of heaven, but 50% of them, half of them, were deceived and lost. Imagine a church of 100 people, where half of them are yet unconverted individuals, or worse, a church of 3,000 members, which 1,500 will go to hell when they die and not heaven because they're just deceived. Dr. R. G. Lee, the former famous pastor of the huge Bellevue Baptist Church in Memphis, shocked the Southern Baptist Convention one year when he announced that he felt only 10% of his people had an experiential knowledge of Christ Jesus, 90% were lost in his opinion and going to hell.

In verse 10 of our text, we see that half of the virgins

were ready and they went in with him to the marriage and the door was shut. The shut door represents the end of the day of grace. It's now judgment time. Where a tree falls, there it shall lay. He that is unjust, let him be unjust still, and he which is filthy, let him be filthy still, and he that is righteous, let him be righteous still, and he that is holy, let him be holy still. When the bridegroom comes back, you'll be too late then, friend, to get saved, because if you're lost, you'll just be damned. Notice how Jesus responds to the unconverted church member.

> *11 Afterward came also the other virgins, saying, Lord, Lord, open to us. 12 But he answered and said, Verily I say unto you, I know you not.*

"But Lord, Lord, I'm not bad enough to go to hell. I'm a good person. I've been a member of a church for 20 years. Lord, Lord, I'm a deacon in a Baptist church. Lord, Lord, I sing to you in the choir each Sunday. You've seen me there. Lord, Lord, I deserve heaven because I've never robbed a liquor store or killed anybody. Lord, Lord, I'm a good Methodist. Lord, Lord, I walked an aisle for you when I was a youth. I repeated the sinner's prayer, didn't you hear me? Lord, Lord, I raised my hand when they asked us who wanted to become Christians." Too late, friend. You're a day late and a dollar short. You've been sitting on a false foundation of an empty religious profession and your day of grace is closed. It's judgment time and you're a day late and a dollar short.

But Jesus answered,

> *21 Not every one that saith unto me, Lord, Lord, shall enter into the kingdom of heaven; but he that doeth the will of my Father which is in heaven. 22 Many will say*

> *to me in that day, Lord, Lord, have we not prophesied in thy name? and in thy name have cast out devils? and in thy name done many wonderful works? 23 And then will I profess unto them, I never knew you: depart from me, ye that work iniquity.*

"But Lord, Lord, I teach a Sunday school class. Lord, Lord, I'm a seminary professor. Lord, Lord, I'm the pastor of a big church. Why, it runs 3,000 on Sunday." No. You'll be too late then, friend. You're a day late and a dollar short, just like the others. The unregenerate cannot get into heaven. You must be born again. The door of grace will be shut against you, just as solid as the door on the ark in Noah's day was closed to the antediluvians once the rain came. It was too late, try as they may, as they clawed at it with their nails and pounded on it with their fists, it was all to no avail. Their destiny and doom were sealed just like your destiny and doom will be sealed if you are not truly born from above and washed in the blood. When the bridegroom returns, it will not be to offer pardon, but to carry out justice,

> *7 ... when the Lord Jesus shall be revealed from heaven with his mighty angels, 8 In flaming fire taking vengeance on them that know not God, and that obey not the gospel of our Lord Jesus Christ: 9 Who shall be punished with everlasting destruction from the presence of the Lord, and from the glory of his power;*

Jesus came into the world doing good. Jesus healed the sick. Jesus gave sight to the blind. Jesus even raised the dead to life. Yet what happened? Men cried, "Away with him," and nailed him to a cross. Look at that blessed man on the cross, friend. Look at that man on the cross. See him there with his arms outstretched beckoning you to come to him and believe on him. Look at that bloodstained Savior for sin as he squirms and struggles under the terrible weight of sin, my filthy sins, your dirty sins. When all is against him, his love flows out to a world of guilty sinners. The cross is the place where men sought to get rid of him but by his death, it becomes the place where his saving power flows out to all who come in repentance, confessing they are sinners and own him as their Savior and Lord. If you've not trusted this blessed Savior, receive him now before it's too late. Soon, He will come in judgment on the world when his anger shall burn as an oven, and then you shall meet him as your judge and you'll stand there, friend, a day late and a dollar short and they'll be hell to pay.

Come to Jesus, friend, and lay your sin-burden down at his nail-pierced feet. What are you waiting for? What are you waiting for, mister? Don't wait until you're better. Come. Come to Jesus. Young lady, come to Jesus for forgiveness of sin. Bring to him your troubles. Bring to him your fears. Bring to him your heartache. Come. Come. He will soon return. Then it's too late. You'll be too late then, friend.

"When I hear the sound of a mighty rushing wind And it's closer now than it's ever been

I can almost hear the trumpet as Gabriel sounds the chord At the midnight cry we'll be going home.

When Jesus steps out on a cloud to call his children The dead in Christ shall rise to meet him in the air And then those that remain will be quickly changed At the midnight cry when Jesus comes again."

SERMON 5

SAM JONES' LAST SERMON SUDDEN DEATH

Preached On: Tuesday, September 29, 2020

Sam Jones has been overlooked by historians but Sam Jones was used of God and his generation to shake entire towns with revival. His Nashville meetings in 1885 turned the entire city upside down as he preached to crowds of 10,000 at a time where he reached 1 out of every 5 citizens of Nashville. His meetings altered the very life of the city. Taverns closed. Crime decreased. Backsliders were reclaimed and thousands were ushered into God's kingdom as some of the biggest sinners in town were remarkably saved.

The Ryman Auditorium in Nashville was built for him to preach in by his most famous convert of that campaign, Tom "Steamboat" Ryman. In America at that time, he was as famous as D. L. Moody. He said more quotable things than any man of his generation, and when he died, memorials were held in 20 cities, and in Atlanta 30,000 people came to view his body as it lay in state at the Rotunda of the Capitol. His last sermon was preached to a men's meeting in Oklahoma City on October 13, 1906. Sam Jones died within 48 hours of preaching this message, dying suddenly while traveling on a train back to Georgia, and it was as if his own sudden death was an exclamation point to his very sermon.

This searching message is void of humor but full of God as the fiery evangelist brings his hearers to the very verge of eternity. Here now is Sam Jones' last sermon entitled "Sudden Death."

I shall talk tonight from the first verse of the 29th chapter of Proverbs. "He, that being often reproved hardeneth his neck, shall suddenly be destroyed, and that without remedy." There is enough in the bare announcement of this text to bring every man of us to our feet with a question; and that question should be this: "Who is the author of those fearful words?" And the answer comes back: The great God, the infinite God, who made us all, whose sleepless eye overlooks us all, the great God who will finally judge us all. Then if God be the Author of those words, each of us should propound another question: "To whom does he address himself in these fearful words?" And there are a thousand persons in this audience who could jump to their feet and say: "Surely God means me. I have been often reproved, often warned, often rebuked. Wagon-loads of sermons have been wasted upon my life and upon my ears. God has multiplied his calls to me and his warnings and rebukes from my cradle up to this hour." And I say to every man present here tonight: "Brother, if you ever weighed a verse of Scripture; if you ever took a verse of Scripture into your heart and conscience, take this one in tonight, "He that being often reproved hardeneth his neck, shall suddenly be destroyed, and that without remedy."

I but announce tonight a fact patent to every thoughtful reading man in this audience when I say to you that there have been more sudden deaths in the last twelve months of this world's history than any twelve months since the evening and the morning were the first day. I but state to you what you can prove to be facts, and I state to you that more men have been swept suddenly and awfully into eternity in the last twelve months than in any twelve months of this world's history by heart failure, by apoplexy, by paralysis, by shipwreck, by railroad disaster, by accidents, by cyclones, by earthquake, by hurricane on the sea, everywhere, and the columns of our papers daily come laden with the sudden and awful deaths that multiply year after year in the pages of human life. You can scarcely pick up one of your daily papers without reading from a dozen to three thousand sudden deaths recorded in its columns, and every sudden death in this line is but a fulfillment of the word of the Lord in this text. We may say what we please, and heaven and earth shall pass away, but not one jot nor tittle of the divine law. God hath spoken it, He hath said: "He- that being often reproved hardeneth his neck, shall suddenly be destroyed, and that without remedy." And God shall bring to pass the fulfillment of his word if he must sweep a nation into hell in the twinkling of an eye. God hath spoken today, and God will fulfill it.

And, brethren, this is a personal message to you. I am talking to hard-hearted, stiff- necked sinners here tonight, that have been preached to from your infancy up to this hour.

I am talking to men and women here tonight, in the range of my voice, that have not heeded ten thousand calls, and are unheeding the reproofs and warnings that have been thrown about you all the days of your life. But God speaks to you in that message. Sudden deaths have multiplied and become so common that we scarcely notice them. We glance up and down the columns of our daily papers, and notice where this score here, and that hundred there, and this thousand there have been swept into eternity since the sun set the day before or rose this morning, until it is so common that it does not attract our attention at all. I say to you, my countrymen, that because it is common it is not noticed, but it is as fearful to die suddenly today as ever; it is as awful to be swept suddenly into eternity today as any day in the world's history. It is as tremendous a fact in heaven and earth for a man to be swept suddenly and awfully into eternity today as it was six thousand years ago. Awful fact! And I propose tonight, with your forbearance and prayers and patience, simply to run over some things that have come under my own observation, and I tell you that which I know, and I tell you another thing that you don't know. This man quit telling lies the day he joined the Church. Put that down! Some of you fellows can afford to lie, but I can't. If I tell a lie, they catch me in it, and prove it on me, and I am ruined and I know it. Some of you little fellows can tell a lie and it don't amount to anything, and nobody will notice it; but whenever I may say a thing you can put my immortality on the truth of what I say. You put that down! For twenty-three years I have never found it necessary to establish the fact that I am sticking to my integrity.

Now, understand that I don't care who doubts it, I don't care who says it is not true; I say it is true, and facts are facts and you can't dodge them. Now, understand that! And I want you to understand that I have no reference to anything said about me in this town. I am talking on general principles; and if you think I have told a lie, you come to my room, old fellow, and I will show you that my lie is the biggest truth you ever heard in your life.

Now do you hear that? You see what I mean? Thank God! I quit telling lies when I joined the Church; and if every fellow in this town had done the same thing, we would have been a heap better off in this world. We would that. I am sticking to facts.

Now hear me: 1 simply relate to you to-night the incidents which have occurred in my own life and under my own experience and observation. And I start in with this proposition, which I want you to take home with you: that this man who is preaching to you tonight has preached the gospel earnestly and faithfully to thousands and tens of thousands of men who, since my voice died in their ears, have been swept suddenly and awfully into the presence of God.

When I was preaching in the most memorable meeting in Nashville, Tennessee ten years ago, the most marvelous in grace I ever looked upon in my life, I believe more men were converted, and more people joined the Church from that memorable meeting, than any work of grace almost in this nineteenth century. It was marvelous to behold at that meeting that grand man, Capt. Tom Ryman, of Nashville, Tennessee, than whom there has been no grander convert to Christianity in this nineteenth century. He came to that meeting as others did; he came up to the altar, knelt down like a little child, and gave his heart to God. The day after his conversion he walked up to me and said: "Brother Jones, I want you to go to my home." I said: "Captain, I can't go before Friday." "Well," he said, "I will be glad to have you then; I want my wife and children to see you, who have won me to God, and will you give me that pledge?" I said: "Yes, Captain, on Friday after the preaching."

On that morning, I went with him over to his home, and when we walked into his elegant home in Nashville he carried me into the parlor, and there were thirteen guests, his friends, gathered in the parlor. He invited them there on that occasion, and he introduced me to them one at a time. We sat down a few moments, and his noble wife came to the door and said, "Gentlemen, dinner is ready"; and we walked across the hall into his dining room and sat down at the long table. He put me at the head of the table, and said, "I want you to occupy that place, the post of honor, sir; take this place here"; and he put his friends to my right and left. Of the four men that sat next to me, two of them, steamboat captains, were immediately to my left; the one immediately to my right was the Mayor of the city, and the one immediately by his side was another one of his steamboat captains, for Capt. Ryman owned several boats plying up and down the Cumberland River.

Just as we crossed the hall going into the dining room he had said: "I have invited my friends to meet you, and whenever a question arises you can put in some word and you can press the question of surrender to God upon my friends as we eat; you might not have another chance to do personal work with them." And I sat there at the table, and as we ate I pressed the great question of eternity upon those men, and especially the four who sat next to me. Now listen: not one of those four men was ever, as I knew, moved at all in that meeting. Now results: I don't think it was three months after I left that town till Capt. Ryman wrote me: "Brother Jones, the steamboat captain who sat immediately to your left fell over on his boat the other day, and was dead when his friends got to him." It wasn't many weeks till he wrote me again: "Another one of our steamboat captains came up the river, came into his home and died suddenly; and his wife and children gathered about him, but he was gone." And he said: "O what a fearful fact that those men wouldn't come to God in that meeting!" It wasn't many weeks until I saw where the Mayor of the city of Nashville was up in Wisconsin out hunting, and his friend's gun went off accidentally and put a great load of shot into his head, and he fell forward, and spoke not another word. It wasn't long after that till Capt. Ryman wrote me: "Brother Jones, the steamboat captain who sat next to the Mayor at the table has been swept suddenly and awfully into eternity "And those four men — whether they were prepared or not, I am not here to say — but those four men who sat next to me at the table all went suddenly into the presence of God. And these are but instances that have occurred all along the line. O, my countrymen, I say that this man who talks to you tonight has pressed the gospel with its weight and power upon hundreds of men who have died suddenly and awfully after the gospel had died out of their ears.

I preached in Charlotte, North Carolina at one of the men's meeting. I pleaded so earnestly; many came forward.

Just before the invitation closed a young, bright-looking fellow in his mid-twenties walked down the aisle. He came more than two-thirds of the way; he turned suddenly and went back. It may have been the scoff of a companion, or the jeer of a friend that turned him — I know not. The next morning, he went down to the depot, for he was a conductor on the Atlanta and Charlotte Air Line. He pulled the bell cord, and about eight o'clock he left. After he ran down the road a few miles he held his train in to meet another passenger train, and there was a freight box standing on the side track, and when the passenger backed against it he was standing behind it, and it knocked him down on the rail, and the wheels ran over him from head to foot, and mashed the very watch in his pocket till it was as thin as a piece of tin; and scarcely fifteen hours had passed from the time my voice had died out in his ears until he was suddenly and awfully called into the presence of God. O what a fact! O what a fact!

Brother Stuart, my coworker, was with me at Palestine, Texas. A man walked those streets with oaths and profanity, and said that Jones was a scourge on any community and a blight, and he said that I was doing more harm than could ever be corrected, and he cursed me upon the street. And when I was preaching the last sermon of that meeting that man fell dead there in that community, and people on their way home from the service found his dead body as it lay helpless upon the ground. And I speak the words of truth and soberness when I say to you that all along through this country where I have preached there have been instances enough to make the devil himself look in horror upon criminals like that. And if you will get the record of those who come to this meeting and hear the words that ought to win them to God, you will find in the history of this congregation instances enough to make your hearts stop beating and your blood curdle in your veins. "He that being often reproved hardeneth his neck, shall suddenly be destroyed, and that without remedy."

I was preaching at High Bridge Camp Meeting, Kentucky, earnestly asking men to come to God. A young, stalwart fellow stood there. He had been listening for fifteen or twenty minutes, and a friend told me afterwards that he turned with an oath from his lips and said that he had had enough of that, He walked right down to the depot and stood but a few moments there when a train ran along. He grabbed at a ladder at the side of the car, missed his balance, and the wheels crushed him, and he was in the presence of God in less than twenty minutes from the time he turned with an oath upon his lips. God have mercy upon men who despise truth, and then die suddenly and awfully! I tell you, my countrymen, you will listen to the word, and you heard what the Lord says. Men may speak things that they cannot bring to pass; but God hath uttered, and the millions that have been swept suddenly into eternity are but attestations to the truth that God will bring his word to pass. You may say what you please, but it is an awful thing to die. You may laugh and scoff at death; but I tell you, my countrymen, it is the most serious hour that ever crowded its issues in on human life. To die! A man leaves his place of business, his store, his shop, and walks up to his home and stands on the front porch of his home just a moment, and then thinks of some kind words he is going to say to his wife and to one of his children, and the first thing you know there is a dull thud on the floor, and the wife runs screaming, and he is gone suddenly

There is a good old, superannuated preacher in my Conference. He is frequently at my home, and he is one of the best men I ever knew And when I am at home, frequently he leads the family devotion, and I scarcely remember the time when he was praying at night that he didn't make use of this expression: "O Lord God, save us this night from sudden death; let it not overtake any beneath this roof." And the old man scarcely ever went over the expression but what it impressed me profoundly. It is an awful thing to die, brother; to die anywhere and anywhen; but it is tremendously awful without a word of warning, a moment to pray or a second to repent. You are gone, and gone forever, into the great beyond.

I don't know where or when or how I will die. I may fall in the pulpit; I can't tell. I may die away from home; I can't tell, but I say this to you: If God will answer my prayer in this and give me the choice of my heart, I would come home some day worn out and tired, and lay quietly down diseased and sick, upon the bed in the family room, and there I would linger for a week or ten days under the kind ministration of my wife and children; I would look upon and enjoy their sympathy and ministrations, and as the days drew nigh and I should bid them good-bye 1 would talk to my wife and talk to each child; I would gather them about me daily, encourage them to love God and live for God, and get home to heaven, and on and on until the last evening came, I would take my children, beginning at the oldest, I would gather them about me and say my parting words; and then, when the doctors had turned their backs upon me and said that my case had swung beyond where materia medica reaches, I would spend my last moments talking to her who has been such a friend to me and who has helped me in all my life. And then, when the last moments came, I would wade down gently into the river of death, and when the river should come up to my shoulders I would reach back and kiss my wife and children good-bye, and go home to God as happy as any schoolboy ever went home from school. But to die suddenly! Without a good-bye, without a moment to commit my soul to God! To die suddenly! It is awful! And awful beyond my power to express it. "He that being often reproved hardeneth his neck, shall suddenly be destroyed, and that without remedy."

I know there are parties in this audience that will go away and say: "I can't be frightened into Christianity; I can't be scared into being religious." Now, brother, let me say this, then: If you are not afraid of death and the judgment bar of God and the awful hell that awaits sinners, you are braver than I have ever been or want to be in this world. If there is anything that ought to rouse a man and frighten him, it is the fact that he is exposed to death and hell, and all that there is between him and eternal wreck and ruin is the fact that his heart beats, and yet it may stop at any moment. "I am not to be frightened into Christianity." Brother, that is the whisper by the graveyard; that is the talk of a coward; for a man to say that he is not afraid of the coffin and the shroud and the grave and the judgment and eternity.

My brethren, let me give you an illustration that we have on that. Into the fated Valley at Johnstown the State sent its civil engineers to examine that dam that held back that lake of waters. They went up and examined the dam. They came back down the valley and said: "We warn the people that that dam is unsafe; some of these days it will break and turn the flood of waters loose upon you." They laughed at those engineers and scoffed at them, and said: "You scare us if you can. It is a trick of land sharks to buy our property at half price. It is not for sale." That fall those engineers went back up there. They examined that dam and said: "We warn you people again; that dam is unsafe and will turn that flood of waters loose upon you." They said: "Scare us if you can. W e understand your project. Our property is not for sale." They went back up there in the spring and examined the dam, and came back down and. faithfully warned the people and said to them: "That dam is cracked from base to top, and we warn yon people it will turn the waters loose upon you." They looked at them and laughed and said: "That's an old chestnut, and it don't amount to anything; we have heard that so often." And it wasn't fifteen days till a man on a fleet horse came loping down that valley with the horse in a foam and sweat from the top of his ears to his hoofs, and as he rode down the valley he cried: "Flee for your lives; the dam is broken and the water is coming." And the people stood on the streets and on their porches and laughed at the horseman and said; "Fool us if you can." But the sound of the man's voice hadn't died out down the street when they heard coming the heaving, sweeping, pouring waters, and in fifteen minutes three thousand three hundred of those poor people were drowned and mangled and buried in the debris down at the bridge below the town. And it took almost six long weeks to dig their putrefying bodies from the fearful pile of debris at the bridge.

Now in my heart I pity a man who despises the warning and turns a deaf ear to the voice that would bring him to peace and to safety. And I am talking to men here tonight who will say: "I am not to be frightened by the cry over these things; I have heard that sort of gospel before." But my brother, mark my words perchance in less than ten days, maybe in less than ten hours, from this moment the heaving, pouring, and sweeping waters of God's judgment will rush upon you, and you will find yourself overwhelmed forever. O, my Lord, help men to heed the warning given them this night! If you ever intend to move your head and heart and repent and believe, God help you to do it tonight!

"He that being often reproved hardeneth his neck, shall suddenly be destroyed, and that without remedy." O what an experience! What an experience! " Shall suddenly be destroyed, and that without remedy!" Remedy! O how we lean toward the faithful physician in the hour of sickness! How he leans upon the effective remedies that he has used so often! O brother, the time may come in your life when the very disease that has struck a vital spot will scoff at your doctor and despise the remedies that he gives. Mark what I tell you. Disease will touch your vital spot by and by, and all the compound remedies of doctors and of the pharmacists will never reach your case. You may have been sick and got well a dozen times, but Death hath an arrow in her quiver that will reach your vital spot at last. We must all die. "It is appointed unto men once to die." We will die once; God help us that we may never die the second death. Amen.

"Without remedy!" I think the saddest hour ever sent to my poor heart was after I had nursed and watched by the bedside with my wife for seven weeks; and on Christmas eve her physician, the one that stood by her almost day and night, took me on my front porch and said: "Jones, I break the saddest news that ever fell on a human heart. Your wife has swung out beyond the reach of human skill, and no remedy in the world now will reach her case." O what a moment that was to me! What a moment! What a moment! O, bless God! in that hour of despair I walked into my upper chamber and knelt down and said: "O God, thou the Father of our Lord Jesus Christ, and thou, blessed Christ, who didst heal the sick and raise the dead when thou wast among men; thou art the same today and forever. O God, intervene now; do for me what no human power can do." And, bless his holy name! she lives today to bless the children of my home and the heart that would have been broken if God had called her hence. Thank God! when human remedies fail we may fall back on the divine arm. O what a fact!

And listen, brother! God says:

"He that being often reproved hardeneth his neck, shall suddenly be destroyed, and that

without remedy." And when that time comes in your case

— and it will come, neighbor — hear me, when your disease will laugh at the doctor and scoff at his remedies, when wife can do nothing and mother can do nothing, and finally when the body is dissolving in death, and the death rattle is in your throat, and your eyes sink in your head, and your tongue cleaves to the roof of your mouth, and your pulseless heart is lying still, when the soul reaches out toward God, and God shall say to you: "No remedy!" In rejecting your salvation forever, you swung out where God himself can't reach you. It is the most tremendous hour that ever came to a human soul: the hour when God himself stands powerless to help and powerless to reach. And God has said it in these words that he who has been often reproved, and hardeneth his neck, shall suddenly be destroyed, and that without remedy. Without remedy here, without remedy at judgment, and in hell to meet its tortures forever! Without remedy! O brother, shall you experience that, just as others have? The hope of your life and heart is to heed the warnings now served out and fly for your life.

My soul is in danger. I will give you a picture at conclusion of this hour, which I would have you take home with you. Hear me, and let every Christian pray that this incident may go into the heart of every sinner. I think the most forcible illustration of the hopelessly wrecked was given to me by Brother Culpepper, an evangelist of my State — and I know no better man who lived in it, or who ever preached the gospel. He said to me: this incident which he related occurred in Georgia, just out from the city where he lived, a little inland town off the railroad. He said to me: Brother Jones, one morning a man came riding into my little town on a beautiful little black pony. The little pony had a bridle and a saddle and all other trappings. The man stopped on the little town square, and began to walk the little animal about as if to emphasize his good qualities, and the people began to look at the pony and to gather about his owner. They wondered and admired the beauty of the animal, and all began to praise it. Presently a little boy about twelve years of age walked up into the circle. One of his friends said: 'Johnny, we're going to raffle for this pony. This man has put him up at fifty chances, two dollars a chance.' Johnny answered: 'No, I don't think it's right; I don't do that sort of thing. I have never done it.' But the other boys began to guy him and said: 'You're afraid; you haven't the money.' And then, the boy's desire getting the better of him, he said, 'I have the money, and I'll take a chance,' and he pulled two silver dollars out of his pocket accordingly. Soon the tickets were all sold, and the raffle commenced. The dice were thrown amid some anxiety and excitement, and when it had ended the man pointed his finger at little Johnny and said: 'Son, it is your pony; you've thrown the lucky number, and you've won.' Little Johnny took hold of the bridle and threw the reins over the little pony's neck and put his foot in the stirrup and mounted. And he was proud as he rode off so gracefully amid the applause of the crowd.

His father, a merchant of the little town, was sitting at the door, reading the morning newspaper, which had just arrived. And he read of an incident which told how a man had a beautiful little pony in the city in which the paper was published the day before. The paper described it as being the most beautiful, but at the same time the most vicious little animal the world had ever seen. It also said, in proof of the assertion, that it had killed no less than four men. And the father just then lifted his eyes from the paper, and, as he did so, he saw his boy on the pony's back. He hurriedly threw the paper on the street and ran to where the boy was. And as soon as he got near him, he shouted: 'My precious boy, get down off that pony! Get down, as life is dear to you! He will kill you if you do not. He has killed four men. He will surely kill you.' But little Johnny lifted up his head, and said: 'O no, papa; he won't hurt me; he's all right now; he's my pony, and he won't hurt me.'

And again the father cried for him to get down. But little Johnny rode off. And presently he passed his own home. His mother and sister ran to the door and cried: 'Johnny, Johnny, get down; that pony has already killed four men; he will kill you; why don't you do as your father asks you, and as your mother and sister ask you?' But little Johnny again lifted his head, and said: 'O, don't fear, mamma! Don't fear, sister! He won't hurt me; he's my pony now, and he won't be vicious anymore.'

And little Johnny rode on. And he rode beautifully for two miles, and then he said to himself: 'I will turn back now and let papa and mamma see how this little pony won't hurt me.' And he turned back. He tightened the reins as the animal began to quicken his pace. But it took the bit between its teeth, and plunged forward beyond all control. And they came to the angle of a road which led to a precipice. And the pony took the road and jumped over the precipice. And when that little boy's parents and friends went to search for him, they found him and the pony crushed to atoms.

There is a young lady on the black horse of worldliness. God, the angels, and good men cry: "Get down! get down! That horse has damned millions." But she says: "O, don't fear; he won't hurt me; I want the pleasure and the enjoyment of the moment; he will not hurt me." Young lady, you will want some day to turn back to God and to heaven. And then, when you take the reins in your hand and tighten its grip, the black horse of fashion and worldliness will take the bit between his teeth, and will rush on and over the precipice of destruction.

There is that young man there. You are on the black horse of profanity. He has landed his millions in hell. God and his angels and good men call on you to get down; they warn you of the fate which others have met. But you say: "No, he won't hurt me. I know just how far to go." But some day when you tighten the reins, when you wish to turn back to God and to heaven, that horse will get the bit between his teeth and rush on to hell with you.

There is that man sitting on the black horse of intemperance. Neighbor, that black horse is leading you over the precipice of destruction into the river of death, which is lined from source to mouth with human wretches. Get down, young man! You say: "O no; I know just where to stop." Some day in the near future, blear-eyed and bloated wretch, as you'll be, you'll take the reins in your hand to turn back to sobriety and to God. But the black horse of intemperance will take the bit in his teeth and run to hell and death with you. Would to God that every man on the black horse of sin would take the lesson to heart!

A preacher in Alabama one night related this black horse illustration incident in his pulpit. And after service, four boys rode off on horseback. One was detained a little. He rode rapidly after his companions. And on reaching them, he said: "Look out, boys! I'm on the black horse." They all rode along about two hundred yards, when suddenly the boy said: "Boys, I've a pain in my head; and, O boys, I've never had a pain like this before.

What a horrible pain! It struck me just a moment ago." He rode on for half a mile with his companions, and just as they had reached a point where the road forked, he said: "Boys, please let one of you ride home with me. I am bad. I do not know whether I'll get there or not." The preacher told me he adjourned the meeting the next day to bury that young man, and thanked God that he had a little time before dying.

God pity the man that is closer to the precipice than that young man! God pity the man that is closest to hell! Take him by the hand tonight, and bring him back to peace, to God, and to heaven.

My message is delivered. I have conscientiously preached the truth to you; may God make it a message of salvation! O take heed! God have mercy on you and may you all be prepared for the day to come!

We are going to hold an after service. Do not go away from here tonight to harden your heart. But stay, you who have been often reproved, and let your heart be softened. Stay and come and surrender yourself to God. Get down off the black horse of worldliness and sin and give your hearts to Him who has died for your salvation. Now we will receive the benediction. May the blessing of Almighty God abide with us now and forever!

Amen.

SERMON 6

WHEN THE HAMMER OF JUDGMENT FALLS

Preached On: Monday, July 1, 2019

Well, gather up close here tonight, friends, so you can hear me better for I have a message you're gonna want to hear because it concerns you. I want to tell you about a man named Noah. This man, Noah, lived in a day where wickedness was all in the earth, very much like our day today. Society today is just as bad or worse than in the days of Noah.

Listen to what God told Noah about how he was through with that generation. In Genesis 6:17 God declared,

17 And, behold, I, even I, do bring a flood of waters upon the earth, to destroy all flesh, ….and every thing that is in the earth shall die.

Now scientists have informed us that it was estimated to be around 750 million people on the earth in Noah's day. That's almost a billion people who drowned and were perished.

That entire generation perished save Noah and his family. It was wiped off the face of the earth.

The title of my message this evening, friends, is "When The Hammer of Judgment Falls." Back in the beginning of my Bible in the book of Genesis in chapter 6, we hear a sound echoing out of the forest. The sound is coming from a man named Noah and it is a pounding sound as he hammered away on that ark. God told Noah to build an ark because God was sending judgment down on that wicked generation. I know you've heard of Noah and his ark, friends, well, listen to the story tonight as I relate it to you. For 120 years Noah obediently hammered away on that ark and he faithfully preached righteousness to that wicked generation of sinners who had no interest in God at all. It was a godless bunch, full of violence and wickedness, very similar to our generation today. Why, you can't go out here tonight without risking being murdered yourself. We live in the most violent society since the days of Noah.

Those evil antediluvians only mocked and made fun of this man, Noah. They made fun of that old white-bearded man named Noah who warned them of a coming judgment every time his hammer fell on that ark. It was to be an ark of safety. They were invited to come in but that generation just laughed and laughed at that crazy old man out in the woods who was building a big boat because it was obvious to anyone with any sense at all that there was no need for it. The teenagers would get together and go out in groups to those woods to watch that silly old man build a boat out in the middle of nowhere, where there wasn't any ocean for hundreds of miles, but the teenagers would come to watch Noah and have their laugh. As they called him names as they mocked him, they'd say, "Hey, old man!" they would yell. They would yell, "Look, it's old Noah, the bearded sailor and his boat!" And Noah pounded away on the ark. As he hammered away on that timber, those antediluvians just grabbed their bellies and just laughed and laughed at such a ridiculous spectacle, and as Noah reached for some more tacking nails, he would cry out to that odd believing crowd of onlookers and he worked preaching righteousness by warning them and he'd start yelling, "Judgment is coming! Judgment is coming!" And he'd go back to hammering away on that ark. "The ark is the only place of safety, I tell you," he'd say. "You'd better be prepared to come into this ark of safety. I tell you, judgment is on the way!" But they just laughed and laughed.

But Noah knew that judgment was coming because God had told him so. In Genesis 6 it states,

13 And God said unto Noah, The end of all flesh is come before me; for the earth is filled with violence through them; and, behold, I will destroy them with the earth.

That generation made fun of Noah as he hammered away on that ark of safety, they just laughed and laughed as they took picnic baskets out there to sit and watch him, to be entertained by him by his crazy talk of a coming judgment and his constant hammering. His message was just foolishness to them. They couldn't see a cloud in the sky. They just mocked and laughed at such a spectacle of an old man building such a monstrosity as an ark when it was obvious to anyone with any sense that there was no need for it.

But God looked down from heaven on that wicked generation whose every step took them closer to judgment – hear me now – took them closer to judgment. Noah building that ark was a warning to a careless world. Every blow of his axes and hammers was a call to repentance – hear me now – every hammer blow was a call to repent but the hearts of men were only set on evil continually, and as God looked down out of heaven and beheld the wickedness of man, it grieved him, it grieved his heart and he said so in Genesis 6,

5 And GOD saw that the wickedness of man was great in the earth, and that every imagination of the thoughts of his heart was only evil continually. 6 And it repented the LORD that he had made man on the earth, and it grieved him at his heart. 7 And the LORD said – hear me now – And the LORD said I will destroy man whom I have created from the face of the earth.

Listen to me, friends, that word "destroy" in the Hebrew language is a significant word. It literally means "to wipe something clean." God was saying, "I will wipe off man from the face of the earth," as if God was going to get out his mop bucket and clean up all the filth that man had done. That generation did not heed the warnings of Noah as he preached righteousness to them and time had run out for that wicked generation for a day came swiftly, a day of judgment came where God brought a flood on the world of the ungodly. Imagine the panic in Noah's neighbors as the skies turned black with thunder; how they hollered as they ran through the forest in the pouring rain, dodging lightning bolts as they fell all around them. The ark loomed before them as their only hope but it was too late for God had already shut the door. Noah and his family were safe inside but they could still hear the screams and the shrieks of the antediluvians who were stuck outside hollering, "Please! Please, let me in!" But it was too late.

Surely had the people of Noah's day believed him and had known in advance what tragedy would befall them, what rains and floods would surround and engulf them, the extent of the raging waters that would drown them and their cattle and all the beasts of the field, that their homes would float and then sink, that they would be helpless to alleviate their entire circumstance, imagine the sorrow and regret that filled their hearts as they were drowning as they did not heed the warnings of Noah and book passage on the ark of safety. Rather they laughed, they mocked and they drowned. Surely had they known all of this, they would have not been so foolish, they would have paid more attention to Noah, they would have become grave and serious and reform themselves and repented before God to avoid such a horrible end as drowning. God even gave that generation a little extra time, he gave them an extra seven days to repent. In Genesis 7:4 we see this is true. We read about this reprieve as God declares,

> *4 For yet seven days, and I will cause it to rain upon the earth forty days and forty nights; and every living substance that I have made will I destroy from off the face of the earth.*

Here God gives a guilty world a reprieve to repent and to turn to him. He gives them seven extra days but the people of Noah's day still did not heed the warning, instead they trifled away those seven days as they sinned even more in their careless attitude and negligent indifference.

Listen to me, friends, maybe there is someone here tonight whom God has been reproving and he's giving you some extra time to repent and to turn to him. Will you be careless as well or will you heed the warnings? That generation of scoffers saw no need for an ark of safety, people today are the same way. They don't see any need of Jesus who is the only refuge from the coming storm of God's justice, the coming storm of judgment from a holy God on sinful man. Today in the land, people go about their normal activities of their day, they eat and drink like they did in Noah's day. They pursued their careers and they saved their money but they cared little about eternity and they are ignorant about the destiny of their very souls that will go out into eternity when they die.

Every one of you here tonight, friends, is an eternity-bound man and woman. Hear me young person, you are eternity-bound. Most folks in this city tonight are consumed by their lusts and full of booze and they just want to sin all they can before the evening is over. They're careless like that generation in Noah's day and they're facing a coming judgment just the same. They seldom think about a final judgment and a burning inferno of a devil's hell. They don't see any need of your Jesus. They don't see any gathering storm clouds and they could care less about a preacher of righteousness today who is here to warn them. God usually warns sinners before he strikes and where his warnings are slighted, the blow will be the heavier. I'm here to warn you, friends, that a storm is coming your way. Repent before it's too late. A day is fast approaching you when judgment will fall.

You don't believe me? Some of you are smiling. I'm just an old man like Noah and I'm pounding away on some sinners tonight with the Gospel of the Son of God and it will be life to some of you and to others it will be death, but I will faithfully preach the full counsel of God to this wicked generation that has no interest in God. My Bible says in Hebrews,

7 By faith Noah, being warned of God of things not seen as yet, moved with fear, prepared an ark to the saving of his house. (Heb. 11:7)

That's the Gospel, friends. In Christ Jesus is deliverance from the wrath to come. Outside of him there is no hope. No hope, hear me now! Listen to me all of you within the sound of my voice as I scream it at the top of my lungs, "Judgment is coming! God must punish sin! Your only hope is to be in Christ, to get under his blood!" All my hope is in Jesus and he's you're only hope too, friend.

There was an echo of a hammer in the woods in Noah's day as he built the ark, and many many years after that there was a sound of a hammer far away in a village called Nazareth as Joseph, the carpenter, made his living hammering away. Standing by Joseph's side was his young son with a hammer in his hand as well as he helped him. The young man was Jesus. Each day, Jesus held that hammer in that carpentry shop working in the craft of carpentry but there would come a day when Jesus would hear the sound of a hammer but it would be in another man's hands as a Roman soldier pounded away on a hammer as he drove nails into the innocent hands and feet of Jesus. They nailed the Son of God to a tree and crucified him there on a hill called Calvary. The sound of the hammer fell announcing a coming judgment upon a generation, and at Calvary was the sound of hammers as well.

That sound of the hammer at Calvary was an announcement to all mankind that God is a God of justice, God is a Judge of all the earth who holds a gavel in his hand. At Calvary, a statement was being made when Christ was crucified. As the Roman soldiers nailed Christ to the cross, every hammer blow that pounded those nails into his innocent hands and feet was an exclamation point that God must punish sin! God must punish sin! God must punish sin! Judgment was about to fall. Jesus on that bloody cross bore the curse, becoming sin for us.

Look at that blessed man on the cross, friend, see his nail-pierced hands and feet. Behold the man. Look at the crown of thorns on that blessed head, his arms outstretched beckoning you to come to him. Listen, friends, judgment is coming. You can't stop it. It's on the way. Every man, every mother's son will one day be judged. God must punish sin. The Judge of all the earth holds a hammer of justice in his hand and it will fall announcing the sentencing of the law to be carried out against you if you are outside the ark of safety. Your only hope, Jesus Christ, for he is the refuge for sin.

Look at those blood-stained hands, friends, look at that blood-stained Savior from sin, the only refuge and remedy for sin. Hear him as he says,

> *6 ... I am the way, the truth, and the life: no man cometh unto the Father, but by me.*

Listen to that man on the cross, friends, as he says,

37 ... If any man thirst, let him come unto me, and drink. 38 He that believeth on me, as the scripture hath said, out of his belly shall flow rivers of living water.

Come to Christ, friend, and believe on him. He is your only hope, the only refuge for sin. Jesus is the ark of safety but you must come to him and believe on him.

When all was against him there at Calvary, his love flowed out to a world of guilty sinners.

10 Herein is love, not that we loved God, but that he loved us, and sent his Son to be the propitiation for our sins.

Hear me, friends, do not reject this Christ, this Christ of the Gospel, this refuge from the coming storm. Jesus is your only hope. In John's Gospel it declares,

36 He that believeth on the Son hath everlasting life: and he that believeth not the Son shall not see life; but the wrath of God abideth on him.

Hear me now – God's wrath abides on those outside of Christ when judgment falls. You must get an interest in Christ, friend, you must come to Christ. The cross is the place where wicked men sought to get rid of him but by his death, it becomes the place where his saving power flows out to all who come in repentance confessing they are sinners and own him as their Savior and Lord. But you must come to Christ, friend, and believe on him.

This is a message of warning to you but it's also a message of hope if you come to Christ Jesus for forgiveness of sins. I'm going to sing a hymn, friends, and if God's been striving with your soul through this message and showing you your need of a Savior from sin, then I want you to come to

Christ for forgiveness for sins as I sing. Listen to me, friends, don't delay. If God's been dealing with you, if his Spirit's been striving with you, remember God gave those wicked antediluvians another seven days to repent and they didn't do anything about it and God swept them away. There may be someone here tonight within the sound of my voice that God is dealing with. Do not delay or he will sweep you away by death. You come to Christ, friend, you believe on him. Get under Christ's blood because Christ's blood can wash away the deepest stain of sin but you must come to him and surrender to a holy sovereign Lord. Give your all to him. Come lay your sin-burden down at his nail-pierced feet.

Look at that blessed man on the cross, friend. He is your only hope. You come as I sing:.

"What can wash away my sin?

Nothing but the blood of Jesus; What can make me whole again? Nothing but the blood of Jesus

Oh! precious is the flow
That makes me white as snow; No other fount I know,
Nothing but the blood of Jesus.

For my pardon this I see— Nothing but the blood of Jesus! For my cleansing this my plea— Nothing but the blood of Jesus!

Oh! precious is the flow
That makes me white as snow; No other fount I know,
Nothing but the blood of Jesus.

This is all my hope and peace— Nothing but the blood of Jesus! This is all my righteousness— Nothing but the blood of Jesus!

Oh! precious is the flow
That makes me white as snow; No other fount I know,
Nothing but the blood of Jesus.

SERMON 7
WHEN DARKNESS FALLS

Preached On: Tuesday, May 14, 2019

Well, I have a very disturbing message to bring before you this evening, friends. It's difficult for me to preach it because of its terrifying subject. It will more than likely trouble some of you who are not accustomed to searching sermons in the pulpits. In America today, stand men who would rather hand you a bomb to soothe your aching conscience than give you better medicine to cure you, to awaken you to your great danger of dying in your sins and being thrust suddenly into the dark inferno of hell.

The title of my message this evening, friends, is "When Darkness Falls," and if you stay with me through it, you may be one who is pulled from the fire. My Bible says, "It is appointed unto man once to die but after this the judgment." The subject of my message tonight is facing death and eternity. Most folks aren't prepared to die and certainly the majority of individuals are unprepared for eternity.

I want to tell you, friends, about a true story. There was a medical doctor by the name of Maurice Rawlings. He was a cardiologist with the UT School of Medicine in Chattanooga, TN who had critically ill patients in the coronary care units of several hospitals. Well, this man, Rawlings, was an atheist who became a Christian when he was confronted with patients who had survived a death experience through resuscitation and they related to him how they had passed into the regions of hell before they were brought back to life by medical technology. This cardiologist said that before he had always viewed death as a painless extinction until he learned from reading the Bible and getting saved that he said, and I quote, "I found it's really not safe to die."

This man, Dr. Rawlings, wrote two books, friends, on the clinical accounts of his own patients who died and went to hell. Maurice Rawlings' first book, which was a bestseller, was called, "Beyond Death's Door," and his second book was called, "To Hell and Back," because that's what happened to his patients, they went to hell and back. Listen, friends, I've read both those books several times through the years and they always disturb me.

He said his patients while clinically dead on the table, their faces would grimace, their eyes would dilate, and when they came back, they would describe the most horrific scenes of hell and its miseries; they would speak fearfully of the hideous faces of demons they saw there in hell.

One lady who died of a heart attack said she was led through a dark tunnel by a big oversized demon while little demons scurried by her feet like hungry rats. One account of a death experience was of a teenage girl who tried to end her life by taking a bottle of aspirin. She went into a coma and once the ambulance got her to the hospital, heart massage was performed on her until she was brought out of that coma, but she kept crying, "Momma! Help me! Make them let me go! Momma, make them let me go!" The doctors tried to apologize for hurting her but she said, "It wasn't the doctors but them, those demons in hell, they won't let me go! Those demons, they want me! I can't get back! Help me! It's awful!" Well, that young lady eventually got saved and became a missionary and she served God with a passion for she knew what hell was like, she'd seen a glimpse of it.

Well, I'm going to give you a glimpse of hell tonight,

friends, to awaken some of you. I'll show you your lost condition because I agree with Dr. Rawlings that for most folks, it's not safe to die for when they come to die, they come up to darkness. When that darkness begins to overspread their soul as they come to the brink of eternity and darkness takes over, it's too late to turn back then as men fall into death, as men fall from a steep hill not knowing where they shall fall as all is darkness, as they tumble down into the bottomless pit of hell itself.

The title of my message this evening, friends, is "When Darkness Falls," and please stay with me while I do my best to bring this message before you, friends, because the devil does not want you to hear it. He will try to distract your attention while I preach it. He'll put other thoughts in your mind while I'm trying to warn you of your great danger of dying in darkness and being carried into the netherworld of hell. You young people, pay attention to me because the devil will keep you on your cellphone so you won't hear a word I say. Hear me now! Your very life is in jeopardy. You could die in a car wreck tonight and your soul could be carried away into eternity, an eternity you are quite unprepared for.

I say carried away, allow me to explain, friends. There is a reliable story about the famous British preacher, Charles Spurgeon. When it came time for him to die, he was in a hotel in Menton, France, and in bed in that hotel room close to death while his aid, Joseph Harrold, was standing in the lobby of the hotel looking out the window while Spurgeon lay upstairs dying, and this man, Joseph Harrold, told the story as true to his own dying day. He said that as he looked out the window of that hotel lobby, he saw in the distance beneath a cloudless sky a bevy of angels hovering in the air as if they were waiting for someone. They didn't have long to wait as the great Spurgeon died within the hour.

My Bible says in the Gospel of Luke that when a believer dies, that angels carry his soul up to heaven. In Luke 16:22 we read, "that the beggar died, and was carried by the angels into Abraham's bosom." I believe that, friends, that when a Christian dies, angels carry that person's soul up to heaven. I also believe that when an unsaved person dies, that demons drag that person down to hell. I believe when you lay dying, a flock of demons will come into your room and crawl by your bedside like crazed hyenas, drooling and salivating for their prey, ready to bust in on you as soon as the door of death is opened, and then to snatch you up and drag you down to a devil's hell.

Some of you may remember the old TV show, "Little House on the Prairie." It was said by a family member of the actor, Michael Landon, that while he was dying in the hospital, he kept flailing his arms around his head in terror trying to push away an unseen presence that would not stop grabbing at him until he died.

When darkness falls on you, friend, where will you go? Where will you go? Will you go to heaven or will you go to hell? You can be suddenly removed from this world without warning, friends. My Bible says in Ecclesiastes,

> *"For man also knoweth not his time: as the fishes that are taken in an evil net, and as the birds that are caught in the snare; so are the sons of men snared in an evil time, when it falleth suddenly upon them." (Ecc. 9:12)*

That's why my message to you this evening is called, "When Darkness Falls," because this darkness of death falls suddenly, friends, when you least expect it.

I came close to dying suddenly last year. I had an appendicitis attack and was rushed to the hospital and when

I came out of anesthesia, I couldn't breathe. I kept hollering, "I can't breathe! I can't breathe!" And they tell me my heart failed and my daughter said I was turning gray as I came close to dying, but God wasn't through with me yet, friends, or I wouldn't be here speaking to you tonight, and I'm here to warn you, to warn you of your great danger of dying in your sins and going to a devil's hell when darkness falls on you.

Believe me, friends, you don't want demons pulling on you to drag you down to that netherworld of darkness and flames. Jesus described hell as outer darkness, a bottomless pit, a place of weeping and gnashing of teeth where the worm never dies, meaning hell is forever. Once you're shut up in there, friend, you can never get out for all eternity. It's a prison. It's a chamber of horrors, friend, that you don't want to go to.

Four things will happen to you and that are certain as the sunrise tomorrow.

1. Your day will come in your life when darkness falls and you are dispatched from this world by death.

2. Your day of repentance is over. It'll be too late then, friend, for there are no second chances for the dead.

3. Your judgment is certain as you face the God of eternity as your Judge and your doom is sealed and read and your sentence is carried out.

4. Your soul will be bound with chains of darkness and cast into a dark hot furnace where flames burn, where the outpoured wrath of God, for you will be locked up in that chamber of horrors called hell.

Hear me now, friends, demons will claw at you like that girl crying, "Momma! Momma, help me! Make them let go of me!" There will be no one to help you, friends, as demons have their way with you in a region of torments that you can never escape from.

Let me ask you, friend, to face the music in your life right now in regard to where you'll spend eternity. Are you saved or are you lost? I want you to do something now, friends, do me a favor right now, friends. I want you to take out a pen and a piece of paper, or take your pen and write it in the margin of your Bible if you have your Bible with you, or write it on your notes in your cellphone, but I want you to write one word, one word that pertains to you: either write the word "saved" or write the word "lost." Do that now, friends. Are you saved or are you lost? If you're lost, wouldn't you want to know it now while you still have time to do something about it? I'd want to know. If I were lost, I'd want to know now before it was too late for me.

Did you write your word down that describes your soul's condition? Did you write "saved" or did you write "lost"? Maybe you didn't write anything. Maybe you're not there yet. Maybe God's still dealing with you and you need convincing. Well, I will continue, friends. Will you die far apart from Christ and enter that region of the damned where lost souls are wailing like banshees with ear-splitting cries across a raging troubled sea?

Listen, friend, when your day is past and it's time for you to die and darkness begins to overspread your soul, it'll be too late then. Once your time of repentance has passed you and God's Spirit no longer strives with you and you cross over that threshold of death, you'll bust hell wide open like a cannonball going through a paper wall.

Turn to Christ, friend, before it's too late. Turn to the Lord Jesus now for pardon for sin as your Savior from sin before you die without him and then face him as your Judge.

Listen to the following pleas from God's word. Hear me now, friends, listen, "Seek ye the Lord while he may be found. Call ye upon him while he is near. Let the wicked forsake his way and the unrighteous man his thoughts, and let him return unto the Lord and he will have mercy upon him, and to our God, for he will abundantly pardon."

Listen, friends, Jesus came to this world to reconcile sinners back to God the Father by dying as a substitute for sin on Calvary's cross. On that cross hung a blood-stained Savior for sin. Look at that man on the cross, friend. He is lifted up from the earth with his arms outstretched to receive you, but you must come to him. Look at those nails in his hands, those nails in his feet. He was fastened on that cross so I could live. Look at that man Jesus on the cross who loved me and gave himself for me. His saving power flows out to all who come in repentance confessing they are sinners and own him as their Savior and Lord.

Listen to him, friends, as he says,

"I am the way, the truth, and the life; no man cometh unto the Father but by me. I am the bread of life. He that cometh to me shall never hunger and he that believeth on me shall never thirst."

Come to Christ, friend, and he has a pure Gospel promise to all who come in sincerity of heart to him for salvation for sin, "And him that cometh to me, I will in no wise cast out."

When darkness falls and it's your time to die, friend, make dead certain you are safe in the arms of Jesus.

I'm going to sing an old Gospel hymn, friend, and if God's Spirit has been dealing with your heart tonight, then don't delay.

Get to Christ who is the Pearl of Great Price. He's worth having, friend. He's worth selling all for so we may be gained. Christ Jesus is the only remedy in refuge for sin.

Don't delay, friend. Don't let him pass you by. Don't let Jesus pass you by. If he's been dealing with you tonight, if the Spirit of God's been convicting you and awakening you and speaking to you, then come to him, friend. Jesus is the friend of sinners.

Listen, friend, as I sing:
"Pass me not, O gentle Savior Hear my humble cry
While on others Thou art calling Do not pass me by

Savior, Savior
Hear my humble cry
While on others Thou art calling Do not pass me by

Let me at Thy throne of mercy Find a sweet relief
Kneeling there in deep contrition Help my unbelief

Savior, Savior
Hear my humble cry
While on others Thou art calling Do not pass me by

Trusting only in Thy merit Would I seek Thy face
Heal my wounded, broken spirit Save me by Thy grace

Savior, Savior
Hear my humble cry
While on others Thou art calling Do not pass me by."

SERMON 8

AN AWAKENED SINNER SOUNDLY CONVERTED

Preached On: Wednesday, July 24, 2013

We live in a day of great spiritual declension and a diluted Gospel. Many are joining churches but few are truly saved. Seldom is a message preached on the vast distinction between a sincere convert and a false professor. The pulpits have made it so easy to come to Christ that very few ever get savingly converted. Therefore, many congregations are made up of a majority of church members who are on a false bottom and rest in a false security. Sadly, many sit in churches in spiritual darkness for want of a faithful minister to warn them to flee from the wrath to come. Because of the gross spiritual decay in the churches, the standard has fallen to such low levels that many are deceived into believing that they are truly converted and on their way to heaven when in reality when they come to die, they enter eternity apart from Christ and awake in a burning hell full of torments and terrors.

Few know how to preach effectively to awaken sinners to their ruined condition. Fewer still, understand the preparatory work of the Spirit of God of conviction and humiliation upon the souls of men before they are truly brought to Christ. Heresy is all around us, hell is open before us and antichrist is soon upon us and it will be too late for the majority of church members in the land who remain in their sins and die apart from a saving knowledge of Jesus Christ.

Allow me to read you an account of a church member who was soundly converted under the preaching of Asahel Nettleton during the second Great Awakening. This account is taken from my biography on Nettleton entitled "Asahel

Nettleton: Revival Preacher." What makes this account so startling is the first hand description of how this man comes to Christ and it is entirely opposite of our modern-day attempts at evangelism that we are familiar with today. The singularity of this account lies in the personal contact that this church member had with Nettleton when Nettleton came to his Presbyterian church in Jamaica, New York on Long Island. Nettleton was suffering illness from a bout with typhus fever and this man drove the evangelist around in his horse-drawn carriage for the frequent rides in the open air were good for Nettleton's health. The year was 1826 and it was a time in America when God was moving mightily in revival and spiritual awakening.

Listen to this man's account as he relates how he came savingly to Christ under Nettleton's powerful ministry. I beg you, listen carefully to the stages this man passes through as the Spirit of God operates on his heart and conscience as he was first awakened to his ruined condition then convicted of his sins, then he passes into a period of true humility and brokenness before coming gloriously to Christ in a sound conversion. Here now are his words. I implore you, friends, to listen to them carefully.

"In perusing the life of Mr. Nettleton, I have had brought vividly to my recollections scenes and circumstances connected with the revival of religion in Jamaica in 1826 of deep interest to me and although more than 18 years have passed, their interest is as deep as ever and I think strikingly illustrates the wisdom and the prudence of that wonderful man in dealing with awakened sinners.

"The first time I saw Mr. Nettleton was on a Communion Sabbath in the early part of the winter of 1826. Two strangers entered the church and walking slowly up the aisle, seated themselves in the front pew. Many eyes were fastened upon them and after service, as is common in the country, many inquiries were made as to who they were for they were evidently clergymen. It was some time before I learned that one of them was the Reverend Mr. Nettleton, the great revival preacher. The church in Jamaica, as is mentioned in the memoir, had been greatly divided. We were literally two bands hostile to each other and bitter in feeling. The Apostle might have said of us, We were hateful and hating one another and there seemed but little prospect of our ever being any better. It was a sad spectacle on that day presented to this man of God.

"When a few days after, I heard that Mr. Nettleton, the revival preacher, was soon going to preach for us I never shall forget my feelings. I determined I would not hear him and especially so when an old disciple, long since in glory, Mr. Othniel Smith who had listened with rapture to George Whitfield 70 years before when he preached in Jamaica, said to me, 'This Mr. Nettleton that is going to preach for us is a most wonderful man. He is said to be the greatest preacher that has been among us since the days of George Whitfield.' He said further that from what he had heard of him, he believed he could almost read a man's heart. So wonderful was his knowledge of human nature.

"I well remember I secretly said, 'He shall not see my heart for I will not let him see me.' So bitterly did I dread anything like close experimental preaching. I had long been a professor of religion, having united with the Rutger's Street Church in 1812 while Dr.

Mildollar was the pastor. And notwithstanding, I had always been outwardly consistent, regularly observing secret and family prayer, constant in my attendance upon all the meetings of the church as well as the public services of the Sabbath as the weekly lecturer and the social circles of prayer and active in all the benevolent operations of the day.

Notwithstanding all this seemingly consistency of character, there was always a fearful whisper from the faithful monitor within that all was not right. There was a secret dread of self-examination and unwillingness to know the worst respecting my case and the idea of coming in contact with a man who would be likely to expose my shallowness if not hypocrisy, I could not endure and accordingly I resolved that something should detain me from church when Mr. Nettleton preached. But although I sought diligently for any excuse, one evening the last plausible, yet I could not find one and contrary to my secret determination, I went to church at the appropriate time with my family.

"After the Sabbath, numbers of the church members called upon Mr. Nettleton at his lodgings to welcome him among us and I was repeatedly requested to do so with the rest. But day after day I contrived to excuse myself although I knew it was a civility that was expected of me. At length, a brother who had often urged me to go, called upon me to know if I would not take Mr. Nettleton a little ride in my gig as he was in feeble health having but just recovered from a protracted illness adding that he found riding not only beneficial but necessary and he knew I could do it just as well as not. I shall never forget my feelings at this proposition. I at first refused outright and was vexed that the proposition should have been made. I treated the brother rudely. He, however, continued to urge and said he had gone so far as to tell Mr. Nettleton he knew I would do it cheerfully. But it was all to no purpose. I did not do it that day but consented to call upon him the next morning with my gig at 10 o'clock if he would be ready.

"The next morning accordingly, I called at the

appointed time and was introduced to him on the sidewalk and never did culprit dread the face of his judge more than I dreaded to be brought face-to-face with a man who it was said could almost read the heart. I received him politely and we soon entered into a pleasing conversation about almost anything and everything except personal religion. This I scrupulously avoided. I found he was in feeble health and somewhat given to hypochondria, therefore, I felt assured I could entertain him by talking about his own ailments. In less than one hour, all my unpleasant feelings had vanished and I felt as free and easy with him as if I was riding with some long-tried friend and that which I so much dreaded became to me at once a source of great pleasure and of much profit.

"The first day he rode with me about six miles and after that for seven months very few pleasant days passed that we did not ride together from 5-25 miles. I became deeply interested in him as a man and as a preacher. Why I at first liked his preaching, I cannot exactly say but I was unwilling to be absent from a single meeting. The class of subjects he chose as his theme of discourse was new. The distracted state of the congregation led those clergymen who supplied our pulpit to select some subjects connected with Christian duty. Brotherly love, if I remember right, was the subject of discourse seven times in about three months. On the contrary, Mr. Nettleton presented the claims of God and the duty of sinners and here I remember we had no opportunity of scrutinizing the sermon to endeavor to ascertain on which side of the division the preacher was. This I considered a master stroke of policy.

"Thus smoothly and pleasantly, comparatively speaking, it passed along with me for about two weeks when one evening he announced from the desk that he felt some encouragement to believe that the Lord was about to grant us a blessing. He said that he had seen several individuals who were anxious for their souls and two or three who indulged hope. How it would end with them he could not say, but he wanted the church to walk softly before the Lord and to be much in prayer. I felt that my own case required looking into at once or I was lost and I resolved soon to attend it, not to let the present opportunity pass. Mr. Nettleton had never yet said one word to me on the subject of experimental religion although I had been with him a great deal.

"The next day, as usual, I called for him to ride. I was obliged to go to Flushing that day, distant about five miles. Just as we were ascending the hill, a little out of the village and before any subject of conversation had been introduced and the horse on a slow walk, he gently placed his hand upon my knee and said, 'Well, my dear friend, how is it with you? I hope it is all peace within.' I could not speak for some minutes. He said no more and there was no occasion for an arrowhead pierced my inmost soul. My emotions were overwhelming. At length, after recovering a little of self-possession, I broke the silence by telling him frankly I was not happy. There was no peace within, rather all was war, war, war.

"His manner was so kind. He instantly won my confidence, and I unburdened my soul to him. I told him how I had felt for years past and how very unhappy at times I had been. He did not seem inclined to talk. All he said was occasionally, 'Well. Well. Well.' with his peculiar cadence. At length, he said he did not feel very well and he wanted to be still. This was a request he often made and I thought nothing of it. I have rode miles and miles with him and not a word has passed between us after such a request.

"I continued to ride with him once and twice a day but

although I was anxious to converse, he said but little to me except occasionally he would drop a remark calculated to make me feel worse instead of better, at times, greatly deepening my distress.

"Some months afterwards, I spoke to him about this part of our intercourse. He said he did it intentionally for he had reason to believe many an awakened sinner had his convictions all talked away and talked into a false hope.

"Two or three days after he first spoke to me on the subject of religion, he called at my house and requested me to go and see a particular individual who he named and who was under distress of mind and pray with her. I told him that I could not do such a thing as that for I was not a Christian myself. He replied, 'But you do not mean that your not being a Christian releases you from Christian obligations? If you do, you are greatly in error. Good morning.' And he left me rather abruptly.

"In the afternoon when I rode with him, he did not ask me if I attended to his request for he knew I had not. He only made the request, as he afterwards told me, to thrust deeper the arrow of conviction and it had the desired effect. My distress became very great and I was unfitted for my ordinary duties. I felt as if there was but little hope for such a hardened sinner as I was.

"About this time, he appointed a meeting of inquiry. I told him I should be there for one. He said I must not attend on any account, it was only intended for anxious sinners. I told him I certainly should be there unless he absolutely forbade it. 'I do,' said he with more than ordinary earnestness. 'Then,' said I, 'you must promise me that you will appoint a meeting for anxious professors.' He made no reply.

"This anxious meeting was the first to be appointed in

Jamaica. It was to be held at the house of a dear friend of mine and one who knew something of the state of my mind. I went there in the afternoon and made arrangements to be concealed in an adjoining bedroom the door of which could not be shut, the bed being placed against it. I was on the ground an hour before the time appointed.

"Mr. Nettleton came soon after to arrange the seats. About this he was very particular. He came into the bedroom where I was concealed two or three times. He wanted the door closed but he found it could not be without disarranging the furniture and he gave it up.

He did not know I was there until some weeks afterwards. The temptations to be present at that meeting I could not resist. Somehow I had received an impression that my salvation depended upon it. I heard so often about persons being converted in an anxious meeting that I thought if I could only be present at such a meeting, that was all that was necessary and, therefore, I was willing not only to run the risk of offending Mr. Nettleton but willing to submit to almost any humiliating circumstances to accomplish my object. I thought it was altogether a piece of cruelty in Mr. Nettleton to forbid my being present and I determined to carry my point privately if I could not openly.

"Situated as I was, I could hear next to nothing as to what was transpiring in the anxious room. Mr. Nettleton addressed those present individually and in a very low tone of voice bordering upon a whisper. When he approached the open door I could occasionally catch a sentence and hear a deep and anxious sob but these words and broken sentences and sobs were loud and pointed sermons to me.

"I wanted to get out from my hiding place that I might give vent to my pent up feelings. In my anxiety, to be released appeared to be greater than it was to be present. At times, it seemed as if I must cry out in bitterness of spirit. So agonizing were my feelings, especially so as I heard him say to one individual, 'Is it possible? Well, I am afraid you will lose your impressions and if you should, what will become of you if the Spirit is grieved to return no more? You will lose your soul.'

"After going around the room and conversing with each individual, he made a few general remarks applicable to all respecting the danger of grieving God's Holy Spirit and then dismissed the meeting after a short prayer. Instead of feeling any better after this meeting as I expected to do, I felt worse and worse. Sleep was now taken from me and I felt that death was better than life.

"Either that night or the next, I forget which but remember it was the 27th of April, I got out of bed about 12 o'clock and went out into the woods. It was exceedingly dark. I fell down at the foot of a tree and cried aloud for mercy in agony of soul. I felt that God was just in punishing me. I felt that the longest and the severest punishment he could inflict was no more than I deserved. My sins, my aggravated sins appeared so great.

"I remained out of doors the most of the night. In the morning, early, before I went home, I called at Mr. Nettleton's lodgings. He sent word that he could not see me at that hour. I went away and returned in an hour or so. He told the servant to request me to be seated and he would be with me in a few minutes. Every minute now seemed an hour and a long one too. For nearly 30 minutes he kept me in this state of horrible suspense during which I was constantly pacing the floor with my watch in my hand.

"When at length he entered the room, I threw my arms around his neck, told him I was in perfect agony and that I should die if he did not in some way comfort me. I told him it seemed as if I could not live another hour in such distress. 'I can't help you, my dear friend. You must not look to me,' and he burst into a flood of tears. 'What shall I do?

What shall I do?' I repeated over and over again in a loud voice. 'You must yield your heart to Christ or you are lost,' said he, and adding, 'I do certainly think your situation a very alarming and dangerous one.'

"After a few minutes he said, 'Come. Let us kneel down.' This was contrary to his usual practice. He made a very short prayer, not more than a minute in length, rose from his knees, advised me to go home and remain in my room and abruptly left me almost overcome with emotion. Had there been any means of self-destruction within my reach, I believe I should have employed it, so agonizing were my feelings.

"He sent word to me by a young friend that he did not wish to ride that day. I passed the most of the day in my room on my knees. Occasionally, I walked for a few minutes in my garden and then returned to my room. It was the just and eternal displeasure of an angry God that seemed to crush me to the earth.

"About the middle of the afternoon, one of the elders came to see me. He expressed surprise at my distress, said there was no necessity for my feeling so bad. He knew there was not. He tried to persuade me all would be well with me soon. I told him that if he could satisfy me, it would ever be well with me. I would gladly and cheerfully endure my sufferings thousands of years. This feeling I distinctly remember, the justice of God and the eternity of his anger distressed me most. I sent for Mr. Nettleton but he excused himself and did not come. Thus, every refuge failed me and all my hopes were crossed.

"It was past the middle of the afternoon and approaching sundown and I had not yet broken my fast. After a short walk in the garden, I again entered my room, locked the door and threw myself prostrate on my settee near a state of hopeless despair as I can conceive a mortal to be on this side of the bottomless pit. I cried aloud, 'O my God! How long? How long? O my God! My God!'

"After repeating this and similar language several times, I seemed to sink away into a state of insensibility. When I came to myself, I was upon my knees praying not for myself but for others. I felt submission to the will of God, willing that he should do with me as should seem good in his sight. My concern for myself seemed all lost in concern for others. Terror seemed all exchanged for love and despair for hope, that God was glorious and Christ unspeakably precious. I was overwhelmingly wondering to myself. The cry of 'Blessed Jesus!' took the place of 'Lord, have mercy!'

"After remaining in my room half an hour or thereabouts, I came downstairs and met my dear wife who had deeply sympathized with me in my distress. I explained, 'I have found him! I have found him and he is a precious Savior!' She was very much overcome. She persuaded me to take some food but I was so happy and so anxious to go to meeting the bell having rung, that I could eat but little.

"I went over to the session house. It was crowded. Benches in the aisles were filled. I obtained a seat near the door. Mr. Nettleton was reading the 211 hymn of the Village Collection:

"Of all the joys we mortals know, Jesus thy love exceeds the rest.

"I thought I never heard so sweet a hymn nor so delightful music. I sung it at the top of my voice of which, however, I was not aware until I saw I had attracted the observation of all near me. My eyes were streaming with tears while my countenance was beaming with delight as a friend afterwards told me. I wanted to tell all around me what a Savior I had found.

"After service, I walked home with Mr. Nettleton and remained with him a few minutes. 'I knew this morning,' said he, 'that the turning point was not far off.' He cautioned me again and again against giving way to my feelings, urged me to keep humble and prayerful and not to say much to anyone.

"That night I could not sleep for joy. I do not think I closed my eyes. I found myself singing several times in the night. In the morning, all nature seemed in a new dress and vocal with the praises of a God all glorious. Everything seemed changed and I could scarcely realize that one only yesterday so wretched was now so happy. I felt it perfectly reasonable that he who had much forgiven should love much. I think I sincerely inquired, 'Lord, what will thou have me to do?'

"And though 18 years have now passed, God is still glorious and Christ still precious to my soul and unless I am greatly deceived, I still pray for a knowledge of my duty and for the grace to do it. I know that I still love to do good and make others happy and of all anticipated delights which I can place before my mind, that of the enjoyment of sinless perfection and heaven is the greatest, but never was a sense of my unworthiness greater than it is at present."

SERMON 9

FIVE REASONS WHY WE SHOULD WITNESS

Preached On: Tuesday, November 4, 2014

I remember a story that Dr. Stephen Olford related to me one day. He said he was riding in a taxicab in New York City and he was witnessing to the cabdriver who asked, "If you are a man of God, why would you want to live in a wicked city like this?" Dr. Olford replied, "Young man, I can tell by your accent that you are a Jamaican. I have often visited that lovely island. Now, let me ask you a question: have you ever seen the white lily that grows in the bog in your native land?" The cabdriver replied, "Oh, yes, mon, that lily is so white as it stands up in that black, dirty bog." Stephen Olford then remarked, "The reason I am in New York City as a minister of Christ is because I am a lily in the bog," and that's what we should be, friends, as believers living in a pagan society. We should be lilies in the bog. We should stand out. We should be a Gospel witness to the lost and be a light in the darkness to a perishing generation that marches blindly to a burning hell. But I fear we are not witnessing as we should. Some do not have a regular witness at all. Some of you haven't shared the Gospel with a lost person in over a year.

But we must be regularly calling men and women and boys and girls to be reconciled to God through our Lord Jesus Christ.

The Apostle Paul declared in 2 Corinthians 5 this very thing in verse 20, "Now then we are ambassadors for Christ, as though God did beseech you by us: we pray you in Christ's stead, be ye reconciled to God." But many of us don't do any witnessing at all. Some pastors feel if they preach on Sunday morning, they are doing their part even if they're preaching to the same group of people every week. But Stephen Olford taught me the importance of a regular Gospel witness, friends. When he was the pastor of Calvary Baptist Church in Manhattan, he would make it a point on Sunday morning to feed the flock with solid expository preaching but on Sunday evenings, he made sure his congregation went out to the highways and hedges and brought the lost in to hear the Gospel presented that evening in a Spirit anointed evangelism approach. Stephen Olford told me he would often walk into a diner in New York City, prop his foot up on the ledge where the stools were and speak to that person about their soul and their need of the Lord Jesus Christ as their Savior. Stephen Olford was a brilliant expositor of God's word but at heart, he was always first an evangelist and every one of you within the sound of my voice should be the same, friend. You have no excuse for not witnessing other than sheer laziness or pride. Laziness because you don't want to get up and get out with some tracts and hand them out to poor lost sinners or pride because you don't want your feelings hurt through rejection. That's it in a nutshell. Listen friends, every single one of us should have an active witness for Jesus Christ in our generation and shame on us if we are not.

Today, I'm going to list five reasons why we should witness to the lost on a regular basis and the title of my message today is "Five Reasons Why We Should Witness." I want us to get out our pens and papers and jot these down as we proceed. First I will list the five reasons, then I will elaborate upon them as we go forward.

1. The Great Commission commands us to be active witnesses for Christ. We will see this in the Gospel of Mark in chapter 16, verse 15.

2. We are guilty of the sin of omission for not witnessing. We are careful not to sin with the sins of commission

but we neglect to realize our sin of omission in not sharing the Gospel with others. We'll have no excuse when we stand before Christ at the Bema Seat of believers for not witnessing for him.

3.   When we share our faith with others, God receives glory due him.

4.   We must warn men of their great danger of dying in their sins and being cast into hell. If we passed a house that was on fire, would we not rush to the door and knock on it and ring the bell and shout, "Fire! Fire!" and warn those inside who were in great danger? Yet we fail to warn men of their great danger of dying in their sins and dropping into hell and its fires.

5.   We should be a lily in the bog to our generation.

Well friends, let's look at this first reason why we should witness and that is 1. The Great Commission commands us to be active witnesses for Christ. This is seen in the Gospel of Mark in chapter 16. You can turn in your Bibles there now. We will be in verses 15-16 and I will quote several Scriptures today so be sure to jot them all down and look them up. Here now is the word of God as seen in the Gospel of Mark. May the Holy Spirit attend the reading of his written word. "And he said unto them." I will stop there, friends, and ask two important questions: who is the "he" that is speaking here? And who is the "them" to whom he is addressing? Why, it's none other than the risen Christ. He is the one giving the marching orders but to whom is he giving them? Is he giving this demand only to his disciples? No friends, his command is to his disciples in each and every generation and that means the Lord Jesus is addressing you and me.

Let us continue with our passage and our duty as

followers of Jesus Christ. "And he said unto them, Go ye into all the world, and preach the gospel to every creature. He that believeth and is baptized shall be saved; but he that believeth not shall be damned." That's a terrible word that our Lord uses here, friends, the word "damned." Oh, to be cast into hell and be damned forever! Listen to what the Psalmist declares regarding those who die without Christ. This is seen in Psalm 9:17, "The wicked shall be turned into hell, and all the nations that forget God." As followers of Christ Jesus, we are commanded to be a Gospel witness to poor lost sinners who apart from Christ will die in their sins and be turned into hell. Oh friends, to be cast into that pit of fire, that smoking hell of misery and flames! Jesus declared, "He that believeth not shall be damned." If only I could walk you, friend, to the rim of hell and lift the lid of that smoking pit of noise and allow you to peer into there, what you saw and heard would keep you up tonight. The cries of the damned; their shrieks of terror and misery. How can we fail to carry out our marching orders of the Great Commission from our Commander, the Lord Jesus Christ? But many of us do. We are too fixed upon the pleasures of this world to think much of eternity.

We'd rather sit in the comfort of our warm home and watch our favorite reality tv show and be entertained by hellish people than go out and reach those who are on their way to hell.

So our **first** reason to witness to the lost is: The Great Commission commands us to be active witnesses for Christ. This leads me to our second reason why we should witness. **2.** We are guilty of the sin of omission for not witnessing. This may shock some of you.

Some only think of sin as something which you avoid like adultery or lying or stealing but those, friends, are sins of commission, things you do. The sin of omission is just as great an offense to God as the other for God hates all sin. Let us see this in the book of James in chapter 4, verse 17 which states, "Therefore to him that knoweth to do good, and doeth it not, to him it is sin."

Let me illustrate this with a story. I was a 16-year-old boy and a friend of my mother's was sick and dying and she asked my mother if I could come over to her house and play my guitar for her, for it made her feel better. My mother told me all this and I refused to go and visit that dying woman and play my guitar for her. I was too busy hanging out with my teenage friends to worry about an old woman who I didn't even know that well and that woman died and when I became an adult, I felt bad about not going and visiting her in her time of need and doing something that would have lessened her pain. It's still painful to me today to think of that great sin of omission in not visiting that sick woman who asked me to come. How much worse is our sin of omission if we fail to go out and tell the sick in soul about a Savior who came down here so we can go up there at the judgment seat of Christ when we stand before Jesus and our life is reviewed and the books are opened. What excuse will we give Jesus for not witnessing for him while we had life in our body and our generation perish into hell? What will be our excuse? "Well Lord, I was busy watching my favorite cooking show on tv and I just couldn't get out and tell folks about you. I was busy at the football game. I was busy on the golf course and I just didn't make the time to share you with others. I'm sorry, Lord, I didn't want to experience rejection by handing someone a tract or telling them about what you did on Calvary and getting my feelings hurt."

Listen friends, when you stand before the one who gave himself for you, who hung naked on a bloody cross because of your wretched sins, who poured out his own blood on your behalf so you could have pardon from sin, what will be your excuse for not telling others about the mercy which you yourself received? What will be your excuse? Your mouth will be stopped because you won't have any excuse and you have no excuse today, friend, for not witnessing for Jesus on a regular basis because if you refuse to do so, it is a sin of omission.

Let me give you some Scriptural examples of sins of omission that are found in our Bibles. Turn if you will to Matthew 23:23 and let me read this striking passage to you which proclaims woe unto you for not doing as you should. Listen to the words of Christ Jesus in his denunciation of the scribes and Pharisees, "Woe unto you, scribes and Pharisees, hypocrites! for ye pay tithe of mint and anise and cummin, and have omitted the weightier matters of the law, judgment, mercy, and faith: these ought ye to have done, and not to leave the other undone." Here now is another example of the sin of omission found in Matthew 25:45, "Then shall he answer them, saying, Verily I say unto you, Inasmuch as ye did it not to one of the least of these, ye did it not to me." Now listen, friends, to this last example found in Luke's Gospel in chapter 12, verse 47 which states, "And that servant, which knew his lord's will, and prepared not himself, neither did according to his will, shall be beaten with many stripes." We know our Lord's will, friends, if we read our Bibles and his will is that we be active witnesses for him while we're on this earth. If we fail here, we fail greatly for we have not done as we were commanded to do by our Lord and Savior, Jesus Christ. The sin of omission in not witnessing should drive us to our knees in repentance before him.

3. When we share our faith with others, God receives glory due him. This is seen in Psalm 96:2-3,

"Sing unto the LORD, bless his name; shew forth his salvation from day to day. Declare his glory among the heathen, his wonders among all people." T

his means when we evangelize and tell others about how God sent his beloved Son into the world for salvation of sinners, then God receives glory from that testimony, friends, and when we proclaim the wonder of Calvary to the lost then God receives glory. The Psalmist says, "Declare his glory among the heathen, his wonders among all people." We tend to think only of ourselves in regard to our Christian service but we must, friends, look at things from God's perspective and from his purpose in the salvation of man. As believers, our chief aim in life should be God's glory and what better way to bring him the glory due him than to tell others of his mercy for sinners. God should be at the center of all our thoughts and all our actions and this includes our witness for him in this sin-soaked world for when we speak to the unconverted about the Lord Jesus and his saving power to reconcile sinners back to God, this in itself honors and brings glory to the Father.

The fourth reason why we should witness is this, friends, **4.** We must warn men of their great danger of dying in their sins and being cast into hell. If we were walking by a house in the evening hours and we saw smoke come out from an attic window, wouldn't we rush to the door and bang upon it with our fists and shout, "Fire! Fire!" to alarm those inside of their great danger? Why then will we not do the same with the poor sinner who is on his way to the danger of hellfire? Why are we silent? Did not someone else tell us about the mercy of Calvary and the Savior who died there?

Allow me to share the following story with you on the reasons why every one of us should be out knocking on doors and handing out tracts and telling folks about Jesus. In the biography of Duane Blue, there is a story which should ignite each of us to go knocking on doors and sharing Christ Jesus with those in our community. Duane Blue relates that when he was in high school, he came home one day and found his mother dead from suicide. He said that there were seven churches in their neighborhood and in all the time they lived there, not one of those church people ever came to their door or to ring it or to tell them about Jesus.

Listen friends, how can we say we are faithful Christians if we are not faithful in our witness for Christ to our generation? I believe a tract ministry is one of the most effective ways to witness on a regular basis. I've handed out tracts for years. I've even written some of my own tracts and had a local printer print up a couple thousand of them. You can buy tracts in bulk from the American Tract Society or from Bible True Publishers in Addison, Illinois. That tract you hand someone will keep on speaking to them long after you have left. I always keep a stack of tracts in my glove box in my car. But whether it's an effective tract ministry or a personal verbal witness, we must get proactive and do this fourth reason to witness which is to warn men of their great danger of dying in their sins and being cast into hell.

The last reason to witness is that we should be a lily in the bog to our generation. Listen friends, we live in a dark hour of world history that is growing more and more wicked every day. It seems at times that our society is one black bog of sin and evil and many are sinking in the mire of sin and need to hear the remedy for sin in the person of Jesus Christ. Our job is to be like Stephen Olford and be a lily in the bog to the community in which we live. We must tell our generation who live in darkness about the light of the world who "was the the true Light, which lighteth every man that cometh into the world. He was in the world, and the world was made by him, and the world knew him not. But as many as received him, to them gave he power to become the sons of God, even to them that believe on his name: Which were born, not of blood, nor of the will of the flesh, nor of the will of man, but of God."

You see friends, we live in a day where the church has committed a great crime by taking salvation out of the hands of God and putting it in the hands of men but it's not the will of the flesh that saves, nor the will of man, but of God. God is the author of salvation. We need to be honest with folks and tell them about the full counsel of God which speaks of man's ruin through sin and his redemption through Christ Jesus and his duty of repentance and his necessity of regeneration. We must be a light and share the truth with folks. We must care for their souls for if we do not share the Gospel with the lost, then we have the following indictment against us like this story I'm about to tell you.

Listen friends, to sin's penalty. "The soul that sinneth, it shall die." Listen friends, to God's mercy in his divine pleadings. "Have I any pleasure at all that the wicked should die? saith the Lord GOD: and not that he should return from his ways, and live?" But if you looked at the church today and the people who comprise the church, it would appear that most folks don't care if the wicked die and go to hell because most folks who are church members today don't witness. I know I've made my blunders in the past by not witnessing to the lost and I'll never forget his face, he was a worker doing some construction work on my house. He was part of a three man crew and he always showed up early and I had to pass time with him while we waited for the other men to show up. But I didn't have much time for him even though he seemed like he wanted to talk every time I saw him. A few weeks later,

I picked up the newspaper and his face stared out at me from the obituary page. He was a young man in his 30s and had died quite suddenly and unexpectedly and he died without me ever bothering to tell him about Jesus Christ. His face still haunts me and his blood is on my hands.

I want to end this message, friends, with a passage from the book of Ezekiel which speaks to each of us here if you call yourself a follower of Jesus Christ. Listen to the striking passage and may it bring conviction to you who need to be convicted of your lack of witnessing and warning men of their great danger of dying in their sins. Here now is Ezekiel 3:18 which speaks of our great responsibility to be faithful witnesses for God to our generation.

> *"When I say unto the wicked, Thou shalt surely die; and thou givest him not warning, nor speakest to warn the wicked from his wicked way, to save his life; the same wicked man shall die in his iniquity; but his blood will I require at thine hand."*

Now friends, I want you to take a moment and look at your hands. Go on. Take a look at your bloody hands. They are witness against you. How can we not warn the wicked to turn from his wicked way?

Today, we have seen five reasons why we should witness but will we do it? Will we do it? People perish all around us while we make our excuses. May God give us the grace to be more faithful witnesses in this area of our Christian lives. Listen dear friends, there are few things more important in this world than the worth of a soul. Let each of us have hearts that care for the souls of men.

SERMON 10

WHEN IT RAINED HELL OUT OF HEAVEN

Preached On: Saturday, July 13, 2019

Well, it's good to be here tonight, friends, and you're not gonna want to miss my message this evening. I want you to hear a story tonight about a man called Lot. Have you ever heard of the man called Lot in the Bible? I know some of you have. I know you have heard of Abraham in the Bible. The Bible talks about Abraham's faith, I know you've heard of Abraham. Well, Lot was a nephew to this man Abraham and they were herdsmen and they had a falling out between them on account of the differences between their herdsmen so they split company and Abraham took the hill country and this man Lot settled in the vale of Sodom because it was a well-watered country with plenty of opportunity, plenty of commerce and material prosperity, but the trouble was Sodom was a very wicked city. In fact, the people who lived there had fallen into such moral depravity and corruption that God took notice of it.

In the book of Genesis 18, God is speaking with Abraham about he had decided to destroy Sodom and God said, "Because the cry of Sodom and Gomorrah is great, and because their sin is very grievous." Well, what cry was God referring to? It was the cry of rape. Sexual perversion had become the primary activity of the men of Sodom whom the Apostle Paul speaks of what sodomy is in Romans 1, "the men, leaving the natural use of the woman, burned in their lust one toward another; men with men working that which is unseemly." In other words, friends, the men of Sodom were homosexuals and they were raping one another and that's how bad things had gotten in this city called Sodom, it had no moral values. The Sodomites had no moral compass and the city was so full of vileness and wickedness that God couldn't find 10 righteous people who lived there to keep from destroying it.

The title of my message this evening, friends, is "When It Rained Hell From Heaven" and this message is about how God will destroy a wicked nation. I believe America has grown wicked like Sodom and Gomorrah. The filth that pours out of Hollywood and the entertainment industry is enough to pollute the entire planet with immorality. In this city tonight, every massage parlor is full, every strip club packed with drooling customers bent on fulfilling their lust before this evening is over. Every gay bar in the city tonight is elbow-to-elbow with customers. There's enough booze being drunk tonight to drown the entire city. Historians tell us that ancient Rome was destroyed because it had become a brothel, America has become one big brothel, there's enough sin taking place in this country at this very hour for God to destroy the entire nation.

America sins all she wants to and then dares God to do anything about it. We see the reason why in the book of Ecclesiastes, we read, "Because sentence against an evil work is not executed speedily, therefore the heart of the sons of men is fully set in them to do evil." That's what was going on in that wicked city of Sodom, the Sodomites' hearts were bent on doing evil. We see this is so in Genesis 19. God sends two angels to Sodom to destroy it and their job is to get Lot and his family out of the city before it's destroyed.

Lot takes the two angels into his home for the evening but the homosexuals of that city saw those two beautiful angels and they wanted to have sex with them. Hear me now

– we call good evil today and we say wrong is right but the word of God condemns all sexual impurity. Soon every Sodomite in town was gathering around the house of Lot and circling it like hungry vultures. Listen to the word of God, "But before they lay down, the men of the city, even the men of Sodom, compassed the house round, both old and young, all the people from every quarter: And they called unto Lot, and said unto him, Where are the men which came in to thee this night? bring them out unto us, that we may know them." In other words, friends, these homosexuals wanted to have sex with those two angels. I'm not gonna honey-coat it, that's what my Bible says and Lot argues with them and said, "I pray you, brethren, do not so wickedly." But America doesn't condemn sexual perversion today, rather America endorses it, legalizes it, and promotes it as healthy normal activity. America has become one big Sodom today. God is ready to destroy the sin-loving nation.

Now these Sodomites standing all around Lot's house decided to get violent because they're burning in their lust and they want fulfillment. We see this in verse 9, what they say to Lot, "And they said, Stand back. And they said again, This one fellow came in to sojourn, and he will needs be a judge: now will we deal worse with thee, than with them. And they pressed sore upon the man, even Lot, and came near to break the door." But listen, friends, to what the angels did next. You see, I'm telling you a story many of you have never heard before because most preachers today are afraid to preach the hard reality of the Bible, that God is a God who must punish sin. Ministers today fear men more than God so they skip over many sections of the Bible which speak about the total destruction of a homosexual city. Some of you are so shocked this is even in the Bible. You go find a Bible tonight, friend, and you go to read in Genesis 18 and 19.

Don't be fooled by churches today who only speak about a God of love and omit the fact that God is a God of justice who is angry with the wicked every day.

Hear me now – some of you may be in grave danger like these Sodomites. Listen to what these angels did next. First they grabbed hold of Lot and pulled him back into the house and then shut the door and locked it. Listen to verse 11, "And they smote the men that were at the door of the house with blindness, both small and great: so that they wearied themselves to find the door." Listen, friends, these lust-filled Sodomites still groped around that door trying to break in to rape those angels, even in their blindness of judgment upon them from God himself, that blindness did not reform them or make them repent, they had become so reprobate in their sins God had no choice but to burn up the city and to destroy them.

That's a vivid picture of men in their natural condition today apart from Christ, they burn in their lust, they are blinded by sin. They are all throughout this town tonight looking for a sex partner. America tonight is blinded by sin as she sins all she wants to right before she faces destruction as well by a provoked God and an offended Sovereign. You can't shake your fist in the face of God, friend, to get by. No sir, a day of reckoning is fast approaching. God will arraign every sinner at a final judgment. There he will cast them into a lake of fire which is an everlasting hell. You don't want to go to hell, friend. I'm here tonight to warn you, don't go to hell. Hell is a terrible place of darkness, fire and smoke and misery. It's a prison from which you can never escape.

Listen to this terrible scene in my Bible of destruction and terror that fell upon Sodom and Gomorrah. Hear me now!

"The sun was risen upon the earth when Lot entered into Zoar. Then the LORD rained upon Sodom and upon Gomorrah brimstone and fire from the LORD out of heaven; And he overthrew those cities, and all the plain, and all the inhabitants of the cities, and that which grew upon the ground." Now listen, friends, to this terrible sight as Abraham watched it in horror from his vantage point up on the mountain. Verses 27 and 28 tell us about it, "And Abraham gat up early in the morning to the place where he stood before the LORD: And he looked toward Sodom and Gomorrah, and toward all the land of the plain, and beheld, and, lo, the smoke of the country went up as the smoke of a furnace."

A furnace!

Now look at this, friends, and listen to me, look this way. Surely had the Sodomites known in advance what utter destruction was about to fall upon them, how that they in their secure and comfortable homes laying together and burning in their lust for one another would soon at the break of day rather than have a pleasant sunrise to greet them and to hear the usual sounds of birds singing to them, rather fire would drop down out of heaven and consume them, burn them up, burn the very flesh off their bones as fiery chunks of smoke and hot brimstone crashed through their roofs and ceilings to consume them in their beds. So great was the sudden judgment from God, so overtaking and consuming in its finality of destruction that the plumes of black smoke billowed up like that of a raging furnace. What a horrible noise Sodom on fire must have made that particular morning, a daybreak filled with the cries and shrieks of the surprised Sodomites as hell rained down upon them from heaven and burned up their city, reducing it to piles of smoke and rubbish. Surely had they know what a horrible and painful fate awaited them, they would have done everything in their power to reform themselves and repent before God and avoid such a final catastrophe, but they had no warning and they perished in an onslaught of falling flames as they were burned to death.

One of the most horrible ways to die is to burn to death. People in burning buildings would rather jump to their deaths than be burned alive. That's what they did in the terror attack on 9/11, they jumped out of the 100th floor to their deaths instead of being burned up. Hell is a region of burning terror and torments. I'm here to warn you, friends, that you must repent or just go on to hell. You are full of the guilt of your sins and you stand under their condemnation of a holy God who must punish sin. Your only hope is to get an interest in Christ Jesus.

Jesus is the only refuge and remedy for sin but you must come to him, friend, and believe on him for forgiveness of sin. Jesus came into the world doing good but wicked men cried, "Away with him!" and nailed him to a cross, but every stroke of the Roman's hammer when the Roman soldiers were nailing up the Son of God, every stroke of the hammer was an exclamation point that God must punish sin! God must punish sin! God must punish sin! Listen to me, friends, look at that blessed man on the cross, look at that blood-stained Savior from sin, his arms outstretched beckoning you to come to him and believe on him. Jesus says, "I am the way, the truth and the life; no man cometh unto the Father but by me." Look at that man on the cross, friend, see his bleeding hands and feet. He cries,

> *"If any man thirst, let him come unto me and drink. He that believeth on me as the Scripture*

has said, out of his belly shall flow rivers of living water."

The cross is the place where wicked men sought to get rid of him, but by his death it becomes the place where his saving power flows out to all – hear me now – flows out to all who come in repentance confessing they are sinners and own him as their Savior and Lord. There's a coming day of judgment, friend, where you will face the Lord Jesus Christ and you will bow your knee to him for at the name of Jesus every knee shall bow. You can come to Jesus now as your Savior or you will one day face him as your Judge. Your Judge! Come to Christ, friend, and get your sins under his saving blood. His blood can wash away the deepest stain of sin but you must come to him and believe on him.

I'm gonna sing a hymn. Listen to me, if God has been dealing with your soul through this message, then don't delay, don't you go to hell, you come to Christ, you come to Christ for forgiveness of sin. Jesus is salvation. He is your only hope. Jesus is the Pearl of Great Price worth selling all for so he may be gained. Come to the nail-pierced feet of that blood-stained Savior and lay your sin-burden down and surrender your all to him. Give your all to him, friend, he can save even you. He has power to save you. You come as I sing.

All to Jesus I surrender All to Him I freely give

I will ever love and trust Him In His presence daily live

I surrender all I surrender all

All to Thee my blessed Savior I surrender all

All to Jesus I surrender Humbly at His feet I bow Worldly

pleasures all forsaken Take me Jesus take me now

I surrender all I surrender all

All to Thee my blessed Savior I surrender all

All to Jesus I surrender Lord I give myself to Thee

Fill me with Thy love and power Let Thy blessings fall on me

I surrender all I surrender all

All to Thee my blessed Savior I surrender all."

ABOUT THE AUTHOR

E.A. Johnston in the Outdoor pulpit at Hanham Mount where George Whitefield preached, courtesy of Digby James.

E. A. Johnston, Ph.D., D. B. S., is a Fellow with the Stephen Olford Institute for Biblical Preaching and is an evangelist and author with eighteen published books. He is the founder of Evangelism Awakening, a revival-based ministry whose focus is the study of historical revival and preaching for revival in our day. He has over two thousand sermons on SermonAudio.com.

SOME OF THE BOOKS BY E. A. JOHNSTON

Many of the following books may be purchased individually or as a set by going to Dr. Johnston's webpage in the bookstore at The Old Paths Publications that has links to distributors. Go to:

www.theoldpathspublications.com/Pages/Authors/Johnston.htm

or

Email us: TOP@theoldpathspublications.com

1. *"A Heart Awake: The Authorized Biography of J. Sidlow Baxter" Foreword by Adrian Rogers (The Old Paths Publications, www.theoldpathspublications.com).*

2. *"Realities Of Revival" Foreword by Stephen F. Olford (Gospel Folio Press, Canada; 2005).*

3. *"No Turning Back" (Gospel Folio Press, Canada; 2005).*

4. *"The Master's Plan: Unfolding God's Blueprint For Your Life" (Gospel Folio Press, Canada; 2006).*

5. *"Know The Book: Bible Survey At A Glance" (Gospel Folio Press, Canada; 2007).*

6. *"Jua Kitabu: Tazamo la Biblia" Know The Book translated into the Swahili by missionary G. I. Harlow (Everyday Publications, Canada; 2007).*

7. *"Walking With God" Foreword by Ted S. Rendall (Gospel Folio Press, Canada; 2007).*

8. *"Return To Me: Entering A Right Relationship With God" (Gospel Folio Press, Canada; 2007).*

9. *"Are You In The Book Of Life?" (Gospel Folio Press, Canada; 2008).*

10. *"Call To Revival" Foreword By Colin Peckham (Gospel Folio Press, Canada; 2008).*

11. *"The Church In Revival" Foreword By Richard Owen Roberts (Gospel Folio Press, Canada; 2008).*

12. *"Olford On Scroggie: Stephen Olford's Notes on the Sermon Outlines of Graham Scroggie" Co-authored with Stephen Olford (The Old Paths Publications: www.theoldpathspublications.com).*

13. *"George Whitefield A Definitive Biography, Volumes 1 and 2 Combined" (The Old Paths Publications: www.theoldpathspublications.com).*

14. *"George Whitefield A Definitive Biography In Two Volumes" (American edition published by Revival Literature, Asheville; 2012).*

15. *"God's Hitchhike Evangelist The Biography Of Rolfe Barnard" Foreword By Bob Doom (The Old Paths Publications: www.theoldpathspublications.com).*

16. *"Asahel Nettleton Revival Preacher" Foreword By John Thornbury, Preface By Richard Owen Roberts (The Old Paths Publications: www.theoldpathspublications.com).*

17. *"Sermons For Revival" (The Old Paths Publications: www.theoldpathspublications.com).*

18. *"A Noble Company Biographical Essays on Notable Particular Baptists in America Volume 11: Portrait of Rolfe Barnard" (Particular Baptist Press, Springfield; 2018).*

19. *"Lectures On Revival For A Laodicean Church," (The Old Paths Publications, www.theoldpathspublications.com)*

20. *"Sam Jones, A New Biography" (The Old Paths Publications:*
www.theoldpathspublications.com)

21. *E. A. Johnston's Book Set, (The Old Paths Publications,*
www.theoldpathspublications.com (30% off retail)

22. *"Revival Trilogy, Three Volumes in One": 1. "Realities of Revival," 2. "Call to Revival," 3. "The Church in Revival," The Old Paths Publications, Inc., www.theoldpathspublications.com*

23. *"How to Have a Dailey Quiet Time," the Old Paths Publications, Inc.,*
www.theoldpathspublications.com

24. *"Going Higher With God," The Old Paths Publications, Inc.,*
www.theoldpathspublications.com

25. *"How to Preach For Revival," The Old Paths Publications, Inc.,*
www.theoldpathspublications.com

26. *"Faith Lessons in A Dynamic God," The Old Paths Publications, Inc.,*
www.theoldpathspublications.com

Many of these books can be purchased in The Old Paths Publications Bookstore at a discounted price. Go here:

https://www.theoldpathspublications.com/Pages/BookStore.htm